Praise for *Knitting the Threads of Time*

"Stitching together bits of knitting history, cultural traditions, and the trials of knitting her first sweater, Nora Murphy has created a gracious, personal account of one of the country's favorite crafts. From Hmong textiles to American Indian weaving, Murphy explores the world's fascination with fiber arts in a multifaceted story that will appeal to knitters as well as non-knitters."

— Diane Wilson, author of
Spirit Car: Journey to a Dakota Past

"Brilliant. We've been waiting since Penelope's time to read history through the handiwork of women."

— Heid E. Erdrich, poet and author of
The Mother's Tongue and coeditor of *Sister Nations:
Native American Women Writers on Community*

"This story of one knitter's first self-made sweater simultaneously weaves an evocative history of knitters reaching across time and space. Deeply felt and broadly researched, personal and universal, Nora Murphy's writing fosters faith in the larger pattern of life."

— Maria Fire, author of *Knit One, Haiku Too*

"Nora Murphy has achieved a finely interwoven narrative consisting of three powerful strands — personal memoir, spiritual reflection, and the craft of knitting as it has evolved through the millennia. This is a skillful and poignant blending."

— Lawrence Sutin, author of
Jack and Rochelle: A Holocaust Memoir of Love and Resistance

"By turns celebratory and meditative, Nora Murphy's narrative connects her experience as a modern mom with the creative work of women and an intriguing history of knitting through the ages. Both lyrical and wry in its observations on love, loss, and the search for self-expression and wholeness, Murphy's book illuminates the meaning imbued in everyday acts of creation, connection, and compassion."

— Katharine Bjork, professor of history and global studies at Hamline University and author of *In the Circle of the Dance*

"A good reminder of the role fabric plays in uniting people across cultures."

— Lee Pao Xiong, director of the Hmong Studies Center at Concordia College

"*Knitting the Threads of Time* is a richly textured exploration of the knitting craft — as a source of warmth, a sign of love shared, and a tangible link to the fiber artists who precede us. This delightful narrative will be enjoyed by knitting pros, novices, and non-knitters alike — anyone who shares the human condition will rejoice in Nora Murphy's insightful prose."

— Bernadette Murphy, author of *Zen and the Art of Knitting*

Knitting the Threads of Time

Knitting the Threads of Time

Casting Back to the Heart of Our Craft

Nora Murphy

NEW WORLD LIBRARY
NOVATO, CALIFORNIA

New World Library
14 Pamaron Way
Novato, California 94949

Text design by Tona Pearce Myers

Library of Congress Cataloging-in-Publication Data
Murphy, Nora.
  Knitting the threads of time : casting back to the heart of our craft / Nora Murphy.
       p.   cm.
Includes bibliographical references and index.
ISBN 978-1-57731-657-2 (pbk. : alk. paper)
1. Knitting. 2. Knitting—United States—Miscellanea. I. Title.
TT825.M788 2009
746.43'2—dc22   2008044944

First printing, February 2009
ISBN 978-1-57731-657-2
Printed in Canada on 100% postconsumer-waste recycled paper

g New World Library is a proud member of the Green Press Initiative.

10 9 8 7 6 5 4 3 2 1

For my parents,
with thanks for the stitches they cast on for me

Contents

Prologue

Darkness Falls

woman sits in her comfy chair. Two needles and a ball of yarn keep her company. She's knitting away at something. Maybe a scarf? Socks? She enjoys the sound of her needles beating like a soft drum. She inhales the smell of the waxy yarn. She exhales the satisfaction of watching a single strand transform into an object of beauty. She is perfectly present, in perfect bliss.

This is not a revolutionary act. It is not a moment to record in the history books. All the same, this woman is a revolutionary. She, and millions of women around the globe like her, are making history in their homes. They are creating clothing for loved ones. They are the grandmother who knits a Christmas stocking for her grandchild, the young mother who stitches a star quilt to honor an elder, the two seventh graders who crochet a baby blanket for a teacher's newborn.

Their craft often has to be wedged into the harried schedules and nonstop demands of modern life. The grandmother knits in the hospital waiting room while she awaits the results of her husband's surgery, his third. The young mother penny-pinches time and money to piece together the dozens of diamonds that will become a star. The preteens' work competes with homework, pimples, and text messages from boys they haven't yet kissed.

What these modern artists often don't see are the remnants of an ancient lineage to which they belong. The grandmother, the young mother, and the girls are all descendants of the women around the globe who have transformed fibers into clothing to protect their families for tens of thousands of years. They are the heirs to goddesses who understood that human survival depends on the cloth. These ancients — from China to Egypt, from Peru to the Pacific Northwest — understood that clothing contains the power of creation. The modern knitter is no different. She too, replicates the act of creation; she too keeps the child, the clan, the community alive.

In North America, most of today's needle artists don't have to worry that our children will go cold if we don't finish the sock, the quilt, or the blanket. We have the luxury of buying most of our clothes at big chain stores at the local mall. We choose freely to make garments. Yet by this choice, contemporary crafters keep the ancient tradition going — a tradition that reminds us of our primal existence on this precious earth, that reminds us where we've come from and who we are.

Inside a stitch, just a single knitted stitch, lies the paradox of the ordinary, everyday textile hero. Her simple stitch helps keep the story of humanity alive; her work casts on stitches for the next generation.

I am a modern-day knitter, though I admit this hesitantly. The domestic sciences have never been my strong suit. I nearly flunked home economics in high school. We started with cooking, but my assignments resulted in burned objects destined more often for the trash can than the table. I didn't fare much better when we started sewing. I loved the idea of making my own clothes, but I couldn't figure out how to thread the bobbin without swearing or slicing my finger. I couldn't cut fabric on the bias. Lacking domestic skills didn't much matter until I had children of my own — children who need three meals a day, every day, who need clothes to keep them warm in the long winter months.

Despite my domestic demerits, I'm the one in charge of my household, which includes middle schooler Andrew, first grader Evan, and my partner and the boys' good friend, Diego. Everyone pitches in: Evan takes out the recycling, Andrew cleans the downstairs bathroom, Diego folds the laundry. Still, under my management, the house is often cluttered, and dinner rarely gets four stars. There's just one domestic art that doesn't stump me — knitting. It's not that I'm very good at it. It just doesn't scare me the way cooking and cleaning do.

Last winter I managed to make wool socks for Evan and Andrew. It had been years since I had knit. I was surprised that none of the basic dance steps with the yarn and two knitting needles had left me. I remembered how to cast on, knit, purl, and bind off without having to think — a bicycle kind of thing. Plus knitting, unlike sewing, has no bias. Knitting welcomes everyone, and the yarn goes any direction you tell it to.

The hardest part of making the boys' socks was deciphering the pattern. If you think that Wall Street or the stock market overuses acronyms, try reading a knitting pattern. MC, BO, AST, and K2P2 are just a few of the abbreviations in knitters' jargon. Whenever I couldn't decipher the sock pattern, I became a rabbinical scholar in training, believing that my new interpretation of the Midrash might clear up a question that had been long debated. My novice knitter's enthusiasm helped me persevere. I reinterpreted the sock pattern again and again until I got it right.

I learned to love creating something from a single strand of yarn. Not just anything. Every mom knows that socks are essential. A mom in the northland knows that warm socks can be critical to survival. I discovered a need to create things for my boys that are functional *and* beautiful. The socks I knit the boys are beautiful, softly curved and sweetly patterned. They are pretty, but not so pretty that they make the boys afraid to wear them.

By midwinter last year, I had knit seven socks: two for Andrew, two for Evan, two for my niece, and a lone seventh sock. I was proud of my handiwork, but even happier that the boys liked their new socks. When Andrew wore them to school, he came home twice saying that he got compliments.

Last winter's sock project gave me so much more than warm boys and compliments. Knitting in the dark season gave me a lookout perch, a space for reflection, and a way to travel back to the heart of what it means to be human. By knitting, I claim my place in the revolutionary act of creation, of survival.

Survival can be a challenge here in the north country. We live in a skinny blue house in Highland, the highest neighborhood in the city of St. Paul, Minnesota. The Mississippi River stretches like a slender yet sturdy string just a mile below our home. St. Paul is not as far north as Anchorage or Stockholm. But still, our city sits halfway between the Equator and the North Pole. Follow the blue 45-degree latitude stripe across a map of the world, and you'll see that St. Paul connects to Harbin in northern China, to Mongolia, and to Sapporo, where Japan first hosted the Winter Olympics. The average temperature in Minnesota in January is 12 degrees Fahrenheit. We get half as much sunlight in December as in June. On the winter solstice, the sun doesn't wake up in St. Paul until almost eight in the morning. It's back below the horizon before rush hour starts in the afternoon.

In summer, five o'clock means the party is just getting into high gear — we've got nearly five more hours of daylight and plenty of playtime to go. In August, we don't think twice about heading out after dinner for a swim at nearby Lake Nokomis (or Grandmother Lake, as the name means in the Ojibwe language). But by mid-October, we pull down the window blinds by five in the afternoon. We're left inside the electric-lit living room staring at each other, wondering how to fill the space between dinner and bedtime.

In many cultures, the darkness makes room for stories told around the fire. My Irish ancestors welcomed the traveling storyteller into their cottage for stories at the peat hearth in the evenings. The Ojibwe, whose sacred tribal touchstone is an island in Lake Superior 150 miles north of here, still tell traditional stories only when snow is on the ground.

My boys get their stories from books and TV. In summer, the light keeps Andrew and Evan outside, and they forget to turn the TV on. But in the dark months, they race downstairs to watch *Malcolm in the Middle* and *The Simpsons*. Warmed by a comforter and the electric heater, they listen to the stories spun by modern bards, like Malcolm's mother, Lois, and that curmudgeon Homer Simpson.

I like to knit in the dark season. With the blinds drawn, I can observe whatever is going on inside. When the boys are in the living room arguing about the rules of cribbage, knitting gives me a chance to sit back and see if they can figure it out themselves. When someone stops by for a visit, knitting opens up a conversation that drifts to daily events and gossip. When Diego gets out his watercolors, I knit, and we share the joy of watching beauty emerge.

Sometimes I knit in silence. This is the silence that comes when the boys are downstairs watching TV, Diego is writing in the studio above the garage, and I don't have to start dinner for another fifteen minutes. This is when the yarn moves by itself. The rhythm of pure energy and creation fills the room until the knitter, the yarn, and the darkness disappear into the radiant light of the heart. In chaos or in silence, knitting opens up space for me to soften and find the brilliant spaces inside the dark.

Inside this darkness, I follow the shafts of light, discovering a mysterious world of connections that pull me back to the time when women first began to make string, to weave, and then to knit. I am no longer only an American mom and novice knitter, but a member of a clan of women who have taken up tools and fiber to sustain their families and honor the earth for millennia. Sometimes the connection is so strong that I want to knit all day, all night, all winter long.

Yet when the days begin to lengthen into spring, I can no longer sit still. I don't want to just observe life; I want to be a part of it. After dinner, I go out into the growing light for a walk in the neighborhood to check on the budding lilacs and the greening banks of the river. Soon it's time to plant the garden, then to weed it. Next come the heat and the harvest that carry us through the full, fat days of September.

When the darkness returns this October, I decide to knit

again. Prompted by my youngest son, I'm going to try knitting a sweater. Along the way, I want to tell a story — the story of *why* knitting for loved ones keeps calling revolutionary women year after year, generation after generation. This winter story unravels the reasons we are making history right here at home, stitch by stitch.

The Back

OCTOBER

Leaves

$\mathcal{O}$ ctober is a bit like the last dance in Minnesota. We know it's the first month of darkness, but we don't want to acknowledge it. We'd prefer to keep our attention on the sunlight dancing off the red and orange and yellow and gold and brown mosaic in the trees overhead. But we know better — a long winter awaits us.

Minnesotans begin preparing for the dark season at the end of October. First, we turn our clocks back to add an hour of light to our mornings. Then we take out our winter gear, like the socks I knit the boys last winter. We put our gardens and our summer flowerpots to bed. Then we rake the leaves, now crinkled and brown, that litter the lawn.

Raking leaves is more than just an annual autumnal activity. It is a ritual in the fullest sense possible. Yes, you have to get the leaves up off the ground, bagged, and deposited at the county compost site; yet a spiritual significance accompanies the action. When you're done, you know with certainty that summer is over. You know it because you have participated in the funeral of all the leaves. You know it because the smell, the sounds, and the texture of both earth and air tell you that death has arrived.

It's a bittersweet ending. No one wants the light to disappear. But in this ending, this death of summer, we create space for something new.

This fall, Diego is recovering from hand surgery, so I convince the boys to join me in the annual leaf-raking ritual. Andrew rakes in the side yard while Evan and I concentrate on the leaves in the front. As I work, I listen to the sound and rhythm of the rake. Scritch, scratch, scritch, scratch. I take big gulps of air, inhaling the last trace of damp earth I may smell for six months. I make patterns in the yellowy grass I find smothered underneath the thick layer of leaves. I offer these leaves silent thanks: the chokecherry leaves that once tempted hordes of blackbirds, the crinkled crabapple leaves whose green once complemented bright pink blossoms, the diamond-shaped leaves of the mountain ash that shaded us through the hot summer months.

"William's grandma knits him sweaters," says Evan while sprinkling a handful of leaves on our leaf pile, like parmesan over a bowl of noodles. "He wears them to school."

"Oh really," I respond, only half listening. "Hey, kiddo, why don't you get the wheelbarrow and fill it with the leaves from Andrew's pile?"

"Okay, Mom," says Evan. Before I know it, Evan and a very full wheelbarrow weave under the rose trellis. He's headed straight for our car, parked out front with the back hatch open. We take armfuls of leaves and throw them into the back of the car. When the wheelbarrow is empty, I inquire, "So, your friend's grandma handknits him sweaters?"

"Yeah," says Evan, smiling at me with his toothless first grader's grin, "just like my socks."

Twenty minutes later, the Honda is stuffed, and both boys need a break. I leave them with super-sized Twix bars and make a first run to the compost site. The drive takes me over the freeway, through a residential neighborhood, past a small university, and finally to an industrial part of the city. I idle in line behind thirty other cars waiting to dump their leaves into a city-wide mountain that will disintegrate into compost for residents and their gardens next spring. I don't mind waiting. My palms are burning from raking, and I love the smell of the dying October leaves in the backseat. Death acknowledged doesn't cause as much pain as death denied.

On the way home, I notice that the clouds are growing thicker in the sky. Rain is on the way. I pass a small knitting store. Borealis Yarns sits on a corner halfway between the compost site and the freeway. It's in a small, brown-trimmed brick building so understated that only the most dedicated knitter could pick it out from the nearby shoe repair shop, coffee shop, and pizzeria. I would never have noticed it had I not been directed there. And I had — by a book on knitting that Diego bought me last winter. Soon after that, we paid a visit to Borealis Yarns to buy a copper stitch holder for that season's sock project.

Today I watch the yarn store disappear out of the rearview mirror. A sweater? I wonder if I *could* knit Evan a sweater. It wouldn't be his first. My friend Elizabeth knit him a striped sweater when he was a baby. When the second load of leaves is ready for delivery, I load up Evan, too.

"You're coming with me, kiddo," I say. "We can stop at

the knitting shop on the way home and you can pick out yarn for a sweater."

"Really, Mom?"

"You bet," I say, happy that the leaf raking is done before the rain hits, happy that during this October ritual of dying, the idea of something new is born — a sweater for Evan.

Beginnings

*B*eginnings are bliss. Think up a new project. Step into a creative world of possibility. This is not the world of rules and structure, like dinner on the table every night by six and, "No, you may not be excused until you finish your peas, Evan." In this world of possibility, you make up your own rules and create a new structure.

Lots of people feel energized, even high, when they're starting a new project. Diego feels this way about painting. Every Sunday morning he hunts down the ad for a nearby crafts store in the newspaper. By ten AM, I can tell by the look on his face that there is a sale on watercolor paper. It is the look of freedom — a freedom that the imagination offers us all.

In knitting, starting a new project means you get to think about what you're going to make, which pattern you'll use, and the colors you'll pick to give the knitted project your own touch. You also decide if you need any extras, like a new pair of knitting needles to get the right gauge for your project. I love all the possibilities. Will it be a sweater or a vest? A cable knit or the traditional stockinette pattern of knit one row, purl the next? Do I need a new tool for my collection, like a circular needle or a longer stitch holder?

The drive to drop off the second load of leaves is extended bliss. I think of Evan's sweater-to-be. I don't yet know the shape, the pattern, or the colors, but I feel the promise of its beauty. In my mind's eye, this unformed sweater holds the possibility of perfection. I am flying so high that I don't even notice that it has started to rain.

While I empty the second batch of October leaves, Evan is reviewing patterns in last winter's yarn book. Twenty minutes later, I park the Honda outside the yarn shop. Before we get out of the car, I turn around to face Evan in the backseat. He shows me the sweater he wants. It's a man's sweater with red-hot flames running up the sleeves.

"Okay, kiddo," I say, without wondering if I can knit such a complicated design. We get out, wait for the light to change, and duck out of the rain into the store.

The inside of Borealis Yarns is a wonderful contrast to its plain exterior. Women and teenagers sit around a large wooden table in the front window, laughing and knitting. Behind them, the walls are covered top to bottom in yarn of every color imaginable. The yarn in this store is not the kind I remember from my childhood — plain worsted wool or acrylic tucked in the back corner of the local drugstore. The yarn here comes in every texture possible. Yarn with fringes, yarn with popcorn balls, yarn with twists, yarn that looks like multicolored dreadlocks.

Evan tightens his grip on my hand and we beeline it for a clerk standing behind an old wooden glass counter. The young woman, who wears a gray cable-knit sweater, takes us to the back of the store to look at some of the yarns we could use. But for details on how to downsize the adult pattern to fit a six-year-old boy, she tells us, we will have to talk to Abby. "She'll be back in a minute," says the young clerk reverentially.

Evan and I enjoy the time we spend waiting for Abby. He loosens his hold on me and observes the people moving around the shop. He is especially interested in a teenager who is hand-cranking a weblike contraption that converts hanks of yarn into more manageable balls. This adolescent helper is wearing fuzzy pink slippers, sweatpants, and a purple pajama top.

Evan pulls me down and whispers, "Is that a girl or a boy?" I can't tell, but I assume that a young person in a yarn shop must be a girl. Between the gender question and the whizzing yarn winder, Evan can't decide where to turn his attention. He wants to float with the wool circling around and around on the metal web, but he also wants to investigate this teenager.

The store is a paradise of color and possibility. The yarns are grouped in mini-cubes stacked high all around the shop. I squint to form patterns with the colors in a section bisecting the middle of the store. I'm drawn to a diagonal stripe of oranges, browns, and golds that remind me of the leaves we've just dropped off at the compost site. Then I spot a new pattern across the aisle. Dozens of red, white, and blue skeins of mohair hint at the American flag. This gets me thinking about other beginnings; beginnings that didn't go well for all parties involved and need to be reworked. Like the beginning of our nation.

For the past two decades I've worked as a writer for community-based nonprofit organizations in the Twin Cities.

I started as a grant writer for Hmong and Vietnamese organizations that served the region's growing population of refugees from Southeast Asia. Later I was asked to do some writing for the Minneapolis American Indian Center. Since then I've mainly written for nonprofits in the Native American community. I have learned more than I have given. My colleagues there have helped me unravel the version of our nation's beginnings that I was taught at school.

As a kid, I learned that our country began with the *Mayflower* and George Washington, with the first Thanksgiving and the Declaration of Independence. An American Indian version of our history reminds us that the continent was not empty when the Europeans arrived. Estimates now put the indigenous population at more than fifteen million in 1492, with over five hundred tribes living all across the continent — from sea to shining sea. The birthplace of the oldest inhabitants of Minnesota, the Dakota, is just down the hill from our house in Highland on the Mississippi River. This is a fact that I did not learn in school.

Diego and I can bike to the Dakota birthplace in ten minutes. If we drive, it takes less than five. The Mississippi River is not a mighty, roaring torrent here, or a gushing deluge of water. It's a quiet stretch of water, not more than a half mile wide. The surface is calm. A small wooded island halfway across this tender channel blocks the view of a second river that runs on the other side — the Minnesota River. The Dakota birthplace is at the southern tip of the wooded island where the Mississippi and the Minnesota meet.

These two rivers flow together all year long — in spring, saturated with mud; in summer, covered in swarms of mosquitoes; in fall, showered in golden leaves; and in winter, dressed in ice and snow. There are always two coming into one, like two knitting needles working together to birth a new piece of clothing.

In 1805, a U.S. army lieutenant from New Jersey named Zebulon Pike came up the Mississippi River to the Dakota birthplace. In less than a year, or so the official Minnesota history goes, the Dakota ceded 100,000 acres of land on either side of the wooded island for $200,000. The truth is that just two of the seven Dakota leaders present signed this treaty and that the Dakota received just $2,000 and 60 bottles of whiskey. Yet our maps name the island Pike Island, not Dakota Island.

Two rivers. Two beginnings.

I know another story with two beginnings, even closer to home. After fifteen years of marriage, I realized that I had adopted a version of myself that was no longer true to my origins. To survive, I needed to leave my children's father and begin again. It requires courage to admit mistakes and start anew. But if we hold stubbornly to illusion, we won't ever find peace.

Starting over is a little like pulling out row after row of a knitting project gone wrong. You have to set down the yarn, pull out the needles, and then watch the piece unravel, stitch by stitch, row by row, thanks to your own merciless tugs at the yarn. At first it hurts to watch one's project, one's story, disappear. You know how much work went into getting this far. Yet, when we acknowledge our mistakes with compassion and alertness, we have the chance to do a better job the second time around. Once the curly wool is free of its former mistaken hold, lightness arises. It's the high that comes with the return of possibility, of beginning. Again.

Shamans

A woman with short-cropped gray hair and glasses enters Borealis Yarns. This must be Abby, the owner of the shop. I can tell by the raspy hello she gives me and Evan that she's a smoker.

"So, you need a little help with a pattern, eh?" she asks in a straightforward manner. Abby points us to two chairs at the front wooden table and continues, "Let me see what you've got."

I show her the flame sweater pattern that Evan has picked out and explain that I want to downsize it to fit him. Evan gives her a half smile. Abby takes the book, holds it up just a few inches from her face, and scours the details of the sweater pattern like a cat getting ready to come in for the kill. Then she leans into her wooden high-backed chair and closes her eyes. The ferocious look disappears. Her middle-aged face is smooth, calm now. I swear she's about to enter a trance. Evan and I stare at her, neither one of us daring to say a thing. Within moments, she leans forward over the table and starts talking — real fast.

"You're going to need to get five stitches to the inch for the arms, so you'll have to use a different kind of wool than this pattern calls for. If you don't switch your gauge you'll end up with a flame going all the way up to his shoulder." Then she turns to Evan and says, "You want your flame to come up to right about here, don't you?" She gently touches his elbow. Evan doesn't answer, but that doesn't stop Abby. She continues, "And when you go to knit the sleeves, here's what you're going to do. You'll cast on forty-eight, but begin the flame pattern on the fourteenth stitch."

I just nod, as if I understand. I don't. Yes, I managed to make it through the sock pattern seven times over last winter, but I am only a novice knitter. The prospect of knitting a sweater that will require alterations terrifies me. I try not to let on, not to Abby. "Can you write that down? Please?" is all I dare to say.

Abby roots around the yarn and books stacked in the center of the table and pulls out a mini–yellow legal tablet and a blue felt pen. She writes as fast as she talks. I try to look over her shoulder to see if I can make out the written directions better than the verbal ones, but she's got her shoulder angled just so, and I can't quite read her transformational recipe.

Next Abby goes to the front window to a big wicker basket filled with hundreds of knitting patterns. She pulls out a boy's sweater pattern and hands it to me. "You'll use this for everything except the arms. Now, let's go pick out the wool."

By now, this knitting goddess has put *me* in a trance. I am willing to follow her anywhere. And Evan is willing to follow me, so we both trail her to the back of the store. Abby first shows us wools that have to be washed by hand. I ask if she

has any that can go in the washing machine. She says sure
and brings us to another tall bin of yarns.

"So, how much does each skein cost?" I venture, not
wanting to upset the master.

"The machine-washable wool skeins are nine dollars
each," answers Abby.

"And how many skeins will I need?"

"With this wool you'll need..." She pauses to do the cal-
culation with her held tilted back again. When she straight-
ens up again, she answers, "About ten skeins."

I wince. "Yikes — almost a hundred dollars for just the
yarn?" I say.

"If you don't mind washing the sweater by hand it'll be a
lot less," says Abby with a smile.

"I don't mind washing it by hand."

We go back to the first bin. She says, "This yarn will only
cost you about forty dollars total, and you can return whatever you don't use if you keep the receipt."

I am falling in love with Abby. Not only is she a whiz
at reformulating gauges and yarn weights, but she hasn't
even tried to gouge me with the more expensive wool. She is
a modern-day knitting shaman, helping knitters navigate
between their ordinary worlds and their dreams.

I first learned about shamans studying religion in college,
but I didn't meet one until I started working at a Hmong
community agency. The Hmong are one of the many indigenous groups in Asia who live outside the mainstream. They
originated in northern China, but because of political oppres-
sion they have moved southward over thousands of years,
some migrating as far as the nations of Southeast Asia.

Most Americans hadn't heard of the Hmong until the
Vietnam War. Even then, we didn't know them by the name

they call themselves. We knew the Hmong as the Montagnards, or mountain people, who lived in the highlands of Vietnam and worked with the United States to fight the North Vietnamese. But the Hmong also lived, and still live, in Laos. During the war, the CIA strategically hired the Hmong living in Laos to destroy the Ho Chi Minh Trail, which sneaked out of North Vietnam into Laos and Cambodia before entering South Vietnam.

The Hmong lost 20 percent of their population during the U.S. involvement in the Vietnam War. Laos is one of the most densely bombed places on earth.

When the Americans left Saigon in 1975, thousands of Hmong refugees poured into the United States. Today, only California has more Hmong than Minnesota. Thanks to the generosity of Minnesotans who sponsored some of the first Hmong refugees in the U.S., the state began attracting large numbers of Hmong moving here both from Southeast Asia and from other parts of the country. The Twin Cities of St. Paul and Minneapolis are home to the single largest urban concentration of Hmong in the country. More than one-third of Andrew's and Evan's peers in the St. Paul schools are Hmong.

Much like the Dakota and the Ojibwe — the two largest indigenous groups in Minnesota — the Hmong have kept their history alive through oral storytelling. Like the Dakota, the Hmong have told the story of their birthplace for thousands and thousands of years. While the Dakota were born of the confluence of two rivers, the first Hmong people emerged from a mountain. But I can't place that mountain the way I can place the rivers that birthed the Dakota. I don't know any Hmong who can, either. That's because the Hmong don't live near this original mountain anymore.

Shamans have played a role in keeping the Hmong people strong across time and place. Nobody chooses to become a shaman: these healers, men and women alike, are called to the task. They find themselves sick, vomiting, and unable to sleep. They feel as if they are going to die. The only remedy is to answer the call to go to the spirit world and accept the task that awaits them there. A Hmong shaman spends years in training and more years answering the questions and concerns that the community brings forward. A dying elder, an unhappy couple, a failing student, a sick infant — these are the day-to-day issues that a shaman can, and must, address. The shaman gathers her instruments and sets off on a journey to the spirit world; when she returns she brings a solution to the family in need.

One of my colleagues at the Hmong community agency was a young man named Bee, whose mother was a shaman. Bee performed another kind of healing — helping fellow Hmong adults find work in St. Paul. He began his job with his smile, and he didn't just smile with his mouth: he smiled with his eyes, and wrinkles of joy would spread across his face like rays of sunlight. He learned his gift of helping others from his mother. When Bee was a child, his mother would disappear at a moment's notice to take care of other families in need, traveling back and forth between the spirit world and the mundane world.

Abby wears all the signs of a shaman on this day of beginnings at Borealis Yarns. She doesn't dress to impress her customers. She's got on jeans and a simple machine-knit black sweater that's made out of acrylic and flecked with gray — ashes, a flake of dandruff, a small tear in the knit, or maybe all three. She isn't in this business to get rich, or she would have started me out at the expensive machine-washable wool.

She doesn't make small talk; she uses her straightforward smoker's voice only when needed. Otherwise, she's comfortable letting a conversation end. Most important, she travels to another world to solve mundane knitting problems here on earth. Abby tilts her head back to help me solve my flame-sweater challenge twice today. When she lifts her head again, she has an answer that I'm sure comes from inspiration or the knitting goddesses, not from the rational, thinking mind.

Abby inspires Evan, too. Under her marvelous gaze, we spend the next five minutes picking out the colors for the sweater. Evan's color combination is stunning. He doesn't want a pure black; instead he picks a charcoal color with minute flecks of light gray. He doesn't want a traditional sun-yellow yellow: instead he picks a golden shade, like goldenrod in late August. He doesn't want a fire-engine red: instead he picks an orangey red, like sugar maples in October.

Abby helps us carry the skeins up to the front counter and turns to her teenage helper. "Alex, here's a crop for you to wind on the machine." To us, she says, "He'll take care of you."

Evan turns and stares at me. The teenager is a boy after all. I wink at Evan. In the midst of this silent exchange, I lose Abby. She disappears to another part of the store, off to solve another knitting challenge, off to make another person's dreams come true.

Casting On

*E*van. Andrew. Cut it out!" I shout as my sons wrestle and throw each other over the top of our living-room couch.

I want to sit quietly in the armchair and start the back, the first of four pieces for Evan's sweater. What I get is two rambunctious boys and a chance to improve my feeble skills in exercising patience.

"Boys, both of you — up to your rooms right now," I yell. It takes three tries, but off they go, up the stairs, each of them saying it was the other one who started it.

We're all feeling a little edgy. The early October days have gone. We've exchanged the golden sunlight of the first half of the month for the dark. And it's been raining steadily for three days. We're stuck inside with one another. Sometimes it's easier to pass our edginess along. Both boys have plenty to pass along. They are having a hard time adjusting to the new fall schedule at school. For Evan, the first grader, it means no more naps during the day. For Andrew, the seventh grader, it means four periods of classes that change every other day.

To survive, we try and try again. It's a little like casting on at the beginning of a knitting project. Sometimes you've got to dig in a little deeper and tease out a new level of patience that you never thought you had. Sometimes you've got to take a time-out. With the boys up in their rooms for ten minutes now, I find breathing room to start the back of Evan's sweater.

After my victorious sock season last year, I expect it will be a breeze to cast on my initial ninety-two stitches for the back of Evan's sweater.

I'm wrong.

I do remember how to cast on — to take a length of yarn and wrap it around the knitting needle and form the first row of stitches — but it takes me several attempts. The first time I cast on, I run out of yarn at fifty-four stitches. I pull them out and start again with a longer strand of yarn. The second time I get my full ninety-two stitches, but when I'm done and look at the stitches, I can see they are uneven: some stitches are too tight, and others are too loose. So I start a third time, feeling more impatient than ever. I slow down. After I form each stitch, I pause to stretch the yarn so that the tension across all the stitches is even. I also make sure that the stitches remain parallel to one another so that the bottom of the sweater won't zigzag.

Once the ninety-two stitches line the size 7 bamboo needle, my impatience recedes a little. It's as if I needed to go through a rough patch so that I could feel good. Why the challenge here at the beginning, when I had been so excited to get started?

The challenges have only begun. As I knit the very first row, I discover that the newly cast-on stitches are tight and stubborn. I have to stab away several times at each stitch before successfully inserting the second needle to form a new stitch. Unfortunately, the second and third rows aren't much easier. There's no energy in the piece yet. There's no flow. I have to create the base, the structure, from the bottom up.

When entering a trance or a deep state of consciousness, shamans and meditators often experience a tightness, a constriction in their bodies. Sometimes they feel they cannot breathe. This tightness is often followed by the sensation of falling. "Like Alice falling down the rabbit hole," one meditator told me, "but when you land at the bottom, you can breathe again. It's actually quite blissful on the other side of the tunnel." The only problem is that to reach this bliss, you've got to jump into the unknown and uncomfortable.

When you live in the north country, the dark, constricted rabbit hole returns year after year. We live with more darkness than light for six months of the year. Casting on and knitting the first couple of rows are like falling down the rabbit hole. It's dark in the tunnel, dark and frustrating. But knitters don't have a choice. We've got to begin somewhere.

I have to understand my limitations, too. I live in the north country with two energetic boys facing challenges as they make the transition to first grade and junior high. To knit my first sweater, there is only one way to go about it — to knit one stitch at a time. I haven't reached the spirit world, like Bee's mother, or like Abby, the knitting shaman. I haven't even landed at the bottom of the rabbit hole like Alice in Wonderland. I'm on my way down the dark tunnel clasping my knitting needles for the bumpy ride ahead.

Old Sweaters

We've had frost the past several mornings. When Andrew heads out to catch the bus at seven AM I lean out the back door, watching him cut across our yard, past the shorn raspberry bushes, and through the neighbor's backyard. When he reaches the alley he stops, turns around, and waves at me.

"Is something the matter?" I ask, pushing the white metal screen door farther open so I can see all of him.

"Look, Mom," he says, "I can see my breath." A perfect cone of steam floats above his face.

By the time Evan and I leave the house to walk to his school two hours later, the air has warmed up. The short walk to school is full of temptations: a squishy white ball tucked at the side of a garbage can, a pair of doves on the telephone wires that run above the alley. His pumpkin patch.

Evan's pumpkins are the jewels of October. The bright autumn leaves are gone, raked up and composted. We're left with monotonous hues of gray and white for the next six months. Pumpkins in late fall are a little like the first crocus in spring. But crocuses are perennials — they bloom every year without any effort after the first planting. Pumpkins require work for five months throughout the season of light. You have to prepare the soil, plant the seeds, water, weed, and untangle the vines until harvest arrives in October.

Pumpkins require consistency and hard work, just like the back of Evan's sweater.

I have finally knit a full five inches of the back piece. After all the fighting with casting on and knitting the first couple of rows, the piece now hangs long enough off the bamboo knitting needles that it is beginning to look like, well, something. It could be a wide scarf, a handbag, a vest, a laptop carrier, or a sweater. What was just a dream has begun to take form. Thanks to Evan's request and Abby's mastery, I am headed toward a goal. Completing the sweater is not a given. But I'm definitely heading somewhere.

Within seconds of admiring my first five inches, self-doubt creeps in. Am I heading in the right direction? So far, the pattern calls for the rib stitch, which is made by knitting two and purling two, over and over again. After a few rows, the piece is starting to look like corduroy, or crenellated towers on a medieval castle. I run my fingers up and down the hills and valleys, wincing as I find a few stitches that are too loose. At least I'm knitting something. It may not turn out to be a sweater, but for now these five inches contain all the possibility of becoming one.

I have worn dozens of sweaters in my lifetime, but my favorite sweater of all time was a mohair cardigan that I got in high school. I bought it in the hip shopping district between my high school and the Mississippi River. In my junior year, a new secondhand shop opened up called Ragstock, which catered to the nearby students at the University of Minnesota. One day I stopped in Ragstock to explore the bins and bins of clothes they organized not by type but by color. Somewhere between the pastel-colored bin of polyester button-down shirts and the discarded bell-bottoms, I pulled out a sweater. It was love at first sight. Its five fat, fluorescent stripes of orange, yellow, lime green, hot pink, and sky blue shouted, "Look at me!" The creamy white edging said, "Take me!" The shiny pearl buttons tempted me: "I'm all yours!"

It was flashy, and I wore it as often as possible — with jeans, with skirts, with sweatpants, with everything. By the time I left home for college in Chicago, this sweater had become my security blanket, my suit of armor.

As a freshman, I lived in a large dormitory called Woodward Court. I felt out of place much of the year. Most of my fellow freshmen were from the East Coast — Park Avenue; Patterson, New Jersey; and Ithaca, New York. The dorm masters, Ira and Pera Wirshup, often joined us in the student dining room for meals. To me, the Wirshups were as remote as the Russian nobility in *War and Peace*, a novel I was assigned to read that year. I imagined them as Count Wirshup, the benevolent ruler, and Countess Wirshup, the difficult but deeply understanding great lady. In truth, Count Wirshup was a professor of mathematics. Countess Wirshup always "had her face on," as my mother would say, and was dressed in something elegant by college-student standards: a necklace with a thick pendant, a silk scarf, a pair of leather pumps, a brooch that sparkled on sunny mornings.

One evening, Eudora Welty came to give a talk in the Woodward Court dining hall. Mr. Wirshup introduced the great fiction writer with few words and a big smile. We all dutifully clapped as a tall woman wearing a dress and a big white sweater took the small podium. I had read a collection of her stories back in Minnesota, and this was the first time I was seeing a celebrity author in person. She read her story about a black piano player in such a soft, lilting voice that I almost fell asleep. Still, when she was done I raised my hand to ask her a question. I wish I could remember my question and the author's answer, but I don't. What I remember is that I was wearing my bright-striped cardigan from Ragstock and that Mrs. Wirshup watched me as my hand waited in midair for the author's acknowledgment.

The next day at lunch, Mrs. Wirshup came up to me at lunch and asked, "Where did you get that beautiful sweater?" Shocked, I just stared. "It's just gorgeous," she continued, now leaning toward me to touch the soft mohair sleeve. "I wonder where it was made."

I hadn't thought to wonder that before, so I tugged at the back of the sweater to read the label.

"Italy," I said. "It's from Italy."

"Wonderful!" she pronounced. "I love it." And with that Mrs. Wirshup was gone. I doubt she ever noticed me again. But the most beautiful sweater in the world had just received her royal seal of approval.

Sometimes I forget to ask myself the obvious. I often rely on people like Mrs. Wirshup to help me ask the questions that lead to deeper truths about the world. But sometimes I can find a good question all on my own. Contemplating my first five inches of Evan's sweater, I wonder, when did sweaters first come to be?

A trip to Diego's writing studio where we keep the 1955 edition of *The Oxford Universal Dictionary* reveals that the word *sweater* was first introduced to the English language in 1529. It meant "one who sweats or perspires." As the word evolved, it also came to signify those who take a sweating bath, or workers toiling away, often at home, for low wages.

I am no sweat-er. Knitting is not the way I make a living. I have made a choice to knit. Sometimes — like when I find casting on difficult or when I find uneven stitches in my work — I wonder why I made this choice. I am not a toiler in a cottage industry trying to survive. I write for a living. I get paid well enough to own a house, buy food, and dress my kids in warm clothes during the coldest months of winter in Minnesota.

I keep scanning the tiny print in the old dictionary for a definition of *sweater* that is more familiar to me. It was not until 350 years later that the word *sweater* acquired the meaning it has today. In 1882, a sweater became "a woolen vest or jersey worn in rowing or athletic exercise; also worn before or after exercise to prevent taking cold."

I share this insight in an email to Elizabeth, an old friend from the days of the Wirshups and their Woodward Court, who later knit Evan's first sweater. She writes back right away and corrects me.

"No," she writes back. "The word *sweater* may be from the 1880s, but sweaters were knit sometime before that, only they were called guernseys or ganseys, sometimes even jerseys or frocks. They originated along the fishing villages of England, Scotland, and Wales where women knit their husbands long-sleeved, water-repellent sweaters to keep them as warm and dry as possible."

I double-check Elizabeth's information and discover she is right. One of the first times that the word *guernsey* appears in the English language is in 1858, when a Cornish newspaper reports on one William Walsh, who has stolen "one cloth coat, one cloth trousers, one cloth waistcoat, one

Guernsey-frock, two shirts, two prints, one necktie and one pocket handkerchief."[1] Photographs of weather-worn fishermen from British seacoast towns in the early 1900s show them sporting somber sweaters knit in one color, nothing as colorful as my favorite striped sweater. Yet these monochrome sweaters feature complicated twists and cables, diamonds and ladders all across the front.

An earlier reference to worsted yarn used to make knitted "men's worsted and yarn frocks" appears in an 1819 advertisement from a shop selling knit goods made on one of the English Channel Islands.[2] However, the British can't claim to have invented the sweater. It seems the people of Scandinavia have been wearing knitted jerseys or sweaters since the 1700s. Scandinavians believe that the British modeled their ganseys or jerseys after the knitted sleeveless undershirts worn by eighteenth-century Scandinavian naval and artillery men.

Guernseys, or sweaters, probably moved to English cities by the 1880s, when they were first worn not by the military or fishermen but by people of leisure — boaters and buxom ladies. A British newspaper advertisement from the late 1880s, which appears in Mary Wright's book on guernseys, features a fashionable woman with a tall plumed hat and a very narrow waist. She is wearing a knitted sweater.

I imagine some of the people across time who probably didn't wear sweaters. Mr. and Mrs. Wirshup's grandparents probably never wore sweaters back in Russia; nor did Princess Mary or Prince Andrew in *War and Peace*. My great-great-grandmother, who emigrated from Ireland to Minnesota in

---

1 Mary Wright, *Cornish Guernseys and Knit-Frocks* (London: Ethnographica, 1979), 12.
2 Ibid.

the 1850s, never wore a sweater. Neither Bee's nor Abby's great-grandmothers wore sweaters. The Dakota and Ojibwe, who lived here long before either Bee's family or mine arrived in Minnesota, never wore sweaters before they met Zebulon Pike and other treaty negotiators.

Evan, on the other hand, will wear a sweater — one with red flames that shouts, "Look at me!" just like the Italian cardigan I once wore. It will be made by his mother, toiling, by choice, in a skinny blue house, not a dark smoky cottage, by the river in a country with at least two beginnings.

Binding Off

This afternoon we have hosted a surprise birthday party for Evan with seven 7-year-old boys at a museum overlooking the Mississippi River in downtown Minneapolis. Both the surprise and the party are a success, yet stressful. I need a break by the time we return home, so I take out my knitting. Whipping through row after row of Evan's sweater back is my medicine.

At ten inches, I add in four rows of his sugar-maple red to form a bold stripe. Then I return to the main color of charcoal gray, this time switching from the rib pattern to stockinette — knit one entire row, purl the next row, knit a row, purl a row. The effect is smoother than on the bottom half of the sweater. I pick up the new pattern with ease, enjoying the longer rhythm of wrapping the yarn in the same direction for the entire row. I'm impressed with how even my stitches look now that I've had eleven inches of practice. When I double-check this time, I don't find any loopy stitches disrupting the tension in the upper half of the back.

I don't want to stop knitting after I put the boys to bed at night. I don't. I'm in the groove. I keep knitting up in my bedroom while Diego and I watch old British comedies like *A Fine Romance* and *Yes, Prime Minister* before turning out the lights. Diego sits in the big armchair watercoloring. I sit on the bed and knit. In no time at all, I'm following the pattern to finish the back piece.

To shape the upper back, I begin by alternately knitting and purling two stitches together at the ends of the rows. Further on, I'm directed to bind off, to finish the top edge by knitting two stitches and then pulling the first stitch over the second one. Soon the upper sides of the sweater back form diagonals, pointing inward like an arrow. These inward angles are where the sleeves will eventually go. By the time I'm within striking distance of the top of Evan's sweater back, I'm down from ninety-two stitches across to just thirty-eight.

The pattern says to save these thirty-eight stitches for later. But how? My brass stitch holder from last winter's trip to Borealis Yarns was the perfect size for a small pair of socks. But it's far too short to hold the remaining sweater back stitches. I improvise. I thread a piece of red yarn onto a fat sewing needle and guide it through the remaining stitches, dropping each stitch off the bamboo knitting needle as I go. Soon there are no stitches left on the knitting needle. All thirty-eight are sitting happily on the red yarn. I make a loose knot so that they can't slip off. The boy's sweater pattern that Abby picked out assures me that I will use these stitches later to knit the neck and finish the sweater.

Now there's one thing left to do for the back of Evan's sweater. I have to cut the back loose from its ball of yarn. I pull out a good twelve to eighteen inches of the charcoal yarn, making sure that I will have enough to weave the loose end into the knitting once I'm done. Then I take a pair of scissors and clip the yarn. I'm left staring at the two end points — the beginning and the end, humble bits of string.

String is where this whole business of making clothes began. Unlike sweaters, which became fashionable only in the late 1800s, the art of making clothes is ancient. One of the oldest of all materials used to make clothes is string.

Historians had long believed that humans did not start making string or textiles until about seventeen thousand years ago. Then, in the 1990s, the archaeologists J. M. Adovasio and Olga Soffer reexamined startling discoveries from two eastern European regions, Moravia and Ukraine. They discovered imprints of woven cloth on 27,000-year-old clay tablets found in Moravia. This means that humans have been weaving and making cloth for much longer than previously believed. It means, too, that the work of cloth making played an important part in our prehistory. To see what this ancient European cloth would have looked like, we have to fast-forward more than ten thousand years to Ukraine, where the oldest known cloth has been discovered. Unfortunately, only small scraps of the Ukrainian cloth survive, leaving us without a picture of what prehistoric Europeans actually wore.

Some images of the clothes women may have worn in Paleolithic Europe were found in the caves of southwestern France. Here, the archaeologists turned to miniature sculptures of women, some two hundred of which have been discovered all over Europe. One such sculpture is the Venus of Lespugue, which is believed to be about twenty-two thousand years old. Carved out of ivory and just six inches high, the figure sports a string skirt that hangs just below her generous hips and buttocks. To me, the French skirt looks a bit like a Hawaiian hula *pau* skirt, but with the fringe hanging only in the back rather than all the way around the waist. Another prehistoric sculpted string-skirt survivor, dating to 20,000 BCE from Gagarino, Russia, has a fringe only in the front. Both skirts, however, are shaped like an inverted pyramid with the pinnacle pointing down, emphasizing the sex of the wearer.

In the past, scholars assumed that the French Venus represented feminine sexual energy. But as more female sculptures have turned up in digs all over Europe, archaeologists are concluding that the female earth goddess wasn't only about sex. The vixen Venus joins sculptures of women shaped like birds, snakes, and frogs. For the controversial archaeologist Marija Gimbutas, the diversity in all these female figurines proves that prehistoric peoples worshipped women and the ever-changing and "eternal cycle of birth, life, death, and rebirth."[3]

For instance, ancient frog-goddess figures found in Europe generally show an enlarged vulva. The figures often sit in a frog-like stance with their legs bent and opened wide. Frogs survive in the mud under frozen lakes all winter long. The female frog images may honor that watery holding place within the womb that is the source of life and regeneration.

Sculptures of women carved in white materials — alabaster or bone — like the Venus of Lespugue, have been consistently found in burial sites. These generally portray a full-figured woman's body, naked, lying straight, with the legs tightly closed. Many burial goddesses have faces carved with birdlike features. In old Europe, birds, and owls in particular,

---

3 Marija Gimbutas and Miriam Robbins Dexter, *The Living Goddesses* (Berkeley: University of California Press, 1999), 42.

were associated with death. Thus these white miniature women likely represent the energy of death.

Not all archaeologists agree with Gimbutas's belief in an ancient matriarchy, arguing that there's not enough evidence to show how figurines like the Venus of Lespugue, in her string skirt, were used. I fall somewhere between the goddess worshippers and the skeptics. Surely this pantheon of prehistoric female sculptures testifies to the many different energies and powers of women. Perhaps they were worshipped as goddesses, or maybe the sculptures simply acknowledged that women's powers are daily constants like the sun rising and the moon setting.

The European female sculpted figurines often appear in ancient temples built from about 5000 BCE. In one temple in Serbia, for instance, there are many birdlike figurines, and so this temple is believed to have been dedicated to death. By contrast, in a temple discovered in Cyprus, archaeologists found mainly figures of women giving birth. Thus this might have been a temple dedicated to birth. Figurines like the Venus in France, with their string skirts, may have been used by women participating in a fertility dance ritual. Images of women dancing in skirts appear outside France, too, and even as far south as Nubia in North Africa.

I am stunned with the idea of a pantheon of women. I can't imagine that there once were temples devoted to them and their diverse powers all over Europe. From my vantage point, that of a twenty-first-century mom in North America, neither a pantheon of women deities nor temples devoted to them seem possible. Perhaps that why I'm not surprised to learn that prehistoric European temples were not huge monoliths standing on top of grand hills. Instead, they were simple houses set alongside all the other houses in the village.

It seems that the daily duties of life were sacred to women, for in these temples, evidence of women's daily work sat right next to the sacred bowls and female figurines that might have been used in worship. The temples contained tools and spaces for women to complete their daily activities, such as weaving and baking. Archaeologists commonly find spindle whorls, ceramic loom weights, and charred remains of wooden looms inside these goddess temples.

Spinning and weaving were both necessary *and* divine. Is it possible, I wonder, to see the divinity in our contemporary cloth making, in our knitting today? I want to cast a length of yarn all the way back to these prehistoric women and watch them at work and in prayer. Yet what string would be long enough to anchor us to these ancients?

Perhaps we're closer to these symbolic female figurines than I realize. The string used to make ancient women's ritual worship skirts was made the same way that we make string — and yarn — today. String is composed of two or three separate strands. First each strand is spun in one direction, and then you put two or three strands together and spin them in the opposite direction.

I look at the charcoal yarn that I've just clipped from Evan's sweater and see that it, too, is made of three strands, or plies, spun together, like the most ancient human string. Sure enough, when I pull the three strands apart, I can see that each strand is made up of tiny fibers that were spun in one direction. The three resulting strands have been spun together in the opposite direction.

The morning after I finish Evan's sweater back, I hop in my blue Honda and head down the Randolph hill. At the bottom of the hill, I turn north and follow the river for several miles. Now that the leaves are nearly gone, the Mississippi comes into clear view. I'm not Dakota, so the Mississippi is not my sacred birthplace. Even so, this river is sacred to me; it is my home base. This liquid string has witnessed all of my life, all of my family's life. It is the umbilical cord that connects us across generations. My Irish great-great-grandparents traveled to Minnesota in a steamboat up this river in the 1850s. Andrew and Evan were born in a hospital overlooking the river. We celebrated Evan's seventh birthday earlier this month at the river, too.

Reaching the end of October is like binding off a piece of knitting. With the leaves gone, I'm back where I started — with a simple strand of string, here at the river.

One down, three pieces left to go.

The Sleeves

NOVEMBER

Flames

"Mom, here's my homework assignment," says Evan, pulling out a piece of card stock from his red homework folder.

I am in the kitchen trying to wash the pot I used to boil potatoes for dinner. I didn't put in enough water, so there's a layer of burned, crispy potatoes at the bottom to deal with. This unwelcome washing-up task is frustrating because the lights in the kitchen are on, but I still can't see very well. This is November, I remind myself. Get used to it.

I keep scrubbing while Evan explains tonight's homework. For the past six years in dark late autumn, Andrew or Evan has brought home a project just like this one. Sometimes the boys have to invent a new flag; sometimes they make mini-books, or do a freehand drawing. But no matter the form, the question remains much the same: "What is a cultural tradition in your family?"

When I was in elementary school, teachers didn't ask us to think about our origins. They taught me that as an American of European descent, this land was my land — Manifest Destiny. It's Pike Island, we were taught, not Dakota Island. Today many teachers work hard to educate their students about diversity in our country. My children are getting a broader view of what it means to be an American than I did. The only trouble I have with this annual assignment is that I don't have any simple answers for my children. Andrew and Evan's ancestry is fairly simple on their father's side. His family is 100 percent English: some of his relatives traced their roots back to the *Mayflower*.

The heritage that I give Andrew and Evan is more complicated. I'm three-quarters Irish, one-quarter Swedish, with a little French mixed in. Trying to find Irish-Swedish-French-American family traditions is hard. It's a little like casting on without any yarn.

I *am* casting on again — this time forty-four stitches for Evan's first sleeve. Fortunately, I have plenty of yarn.

After the dishes are done, I make my way to my chair by the fire and begin the first sleeve. I cast on with the sugar-maple red yarn to match the edging along the back piece. Then I knit four rows for the cuff in the rib stitch — knit two, purl two. At the fifth row, I switch and knit two rows of simple stockinette in charcoal gray.

I dread what comes next — the flame pattern.

I pull out shaman and master knitter Abby's directions for downsizing the sleeves to fit Evan, with explicit orders to knit fourteen stitches in charcoal and then to knit the fifteenth stitch in red to start the flame pattern. I couldn't understand Abby a month ago, but today, as I stare at the notes from her yellow legal pad, I think I get it. Between her directions, a detailed graph of the flame in the knitting book, and my now more nimble fingers, I'm willing to give it a try.

Sliding his homework onto the coffee table, Evan plops down on the couch next to me. We are both staring at the knitting needle that I hold in my right hand and the three balls of gold, red, and charcoal gray yarn that I'm trying to hold in my left hand. Abby's directions and the three balls are egging me on. "Come and get us," they say. But I lose my confidence and find myself caught in cognitive dissonance. I can read the directions, but my fingers don't know what to do. I just stare back and forth between the pattern in the book and the knitting needles, waiting for either my brain or my hands to take over.

Evan breaks the silence by announcing that he'd rather learn how to knit than to do his homework. I welcome the distraction. I set down the six-rowed sleeve and cast a thick purple yarn onto a pair of comfortable knitting needles fashioned from lead-free pencils. One row, one color. I do the first horrid two rows for him, showing him slowly how to form each stitch. Evan is ready to take over before I am ready to let him.

"Mom, let me do it," he says, grabbing for the needles.

His annual November culture assignment mirrors a question that I've been asking myself for the past decade: "What are my cultural traditions?" I haven't found an answer yet, partly because my Irish ancestors, who gave me my biggest chunk of genes, didn't leave many traces of their cultural heritage. There's an old Irish story that explains what I mean.

Once upon a time, an Irish hero named Cuchulainn was studying in Scotland. He built a bridge of giant boulders home to Ireland and challenged the great Finn MacCool to a battle. Finn MacCool was also a revered Irish hero, but he was smaller than Cuchulainn. Finn realized he would have to devise a plan to outsmart his larger foe. By the time

Cuchulainn crossed the rock causeway to Finn's village, Finn was ready. He had dressed up like a baby. When Cuchulainn arrived in the village, Finn's wife introduced Cuchulainn to her son, the "wee lad." As soon as Cuchulainn saw the size of Finn's "baby," he ran back to Scotland in terror, pulling out every boulder along the way. Hardly a trace of that sea bridge remains.

For me, the pathway back to Ireland is like Cuchulainn's causeway, largely hidden from sight. The language, the festivals, the mountains, and the waterways where my ancestors emerged into being are unknown to me. I'm left with a feeling of isolation. Cuchulainn isolated himself physically by choice. My ancestors isolated themselves from the mainland, too. I've only come to understand the emptiness I feel when I see it in reverse. When I attend an American Indian powwow or a Hmong New Year's celebration, I can see communal ties binding a group of people to their collective past. I long for that kind of connection, not only for myself but also for my boys.

Now and again I stumble upon a cultural tie to Ireland, an occasional rock still left undisturbed after all these years. This time of year is a sacred time for the Irish. The Irish believe that as October closes and November arrives, there is an opening between this world and the spirit world. Our dead ancestors make their way through that opening and visit those still living here on earth. Traces of Samhain — the name the Irish pagans used for this time of year — are found in America. Halloween takes its roots from the Irish traditions of Samhain, dressing up in costumes and carving vegetables into masks to scare away unwelcome spirits.

Before Evan was born, I took Andrew to an American Samhain celebration at a hilly, oak-studded park in St. Paul.

We followed the call of a piper to a huge bonfire. Rising 10 to 15 feet in the air, the flames embraced the ancestral spirits encircling us in the dark. It's hard to describe what I felt at that fire — it was an intuitive, "gut" moment when you are certain that something beyond the rational mind is at work. I felt as though I were no longer rooted only in my physical body but part of a larger spiritual body that broke the ordinary laws of space and time. The flames were calling me home, across the ocean to my ancestors in Ireland.

Tonight, the much smaller flame in Evan's sweater arm begins to encourage me in a different way. Once Evan begins knitting on his own, I return to the sleeve and find that I am suddenly following Abby's directions with ease. Though three narrow rows of knitting with charcoal, red, and goldenrod yellow have taken me almost an hour, I'm adjusting to the feeling of twisting the yarn at the back. I can see there are holes or gaps where I've woven in the red and the yellow. I keep on knitting, knowing that eventually I will unravel this first unskillful attempt at the red flame and try again. I need all the practice I can get.

"It's bedtime, kiddo," I say, stretching and standing up. Evan has been knitting steadily, too. His stitches are uneven and many have been dropped, but he's getting the hang of it. I lean over the couch to watch him, correcting him until he has at last finished his row.

After Evan is asleep, I think more about passing on cultural traditions: traditions like language and Samhain, traditions like knitting. It happens in small ways, just as it did tonight. A child imitates a mother. In response, the mother leans over to guide her child. But what about creating a new cultural tradition? Who's the innovator — the mother, the child, or both?

After thousands of years of weaving clothing with vegetable fibers, what mother decided to switch from weaving
vegetable fibers to weaving wool? Perhaps an ancient mother
felt frustrated with the constant dampness of her flax skirt,
chafing her legs. Maybe, having to weave a new skirt because
her old skirt no longer fit after the birth of her child, she
wanted a new look.

Or perhaps her child was the innovator. Imagine a tod-
dler running after a wild sheep and pulling out a clump of the
animal's long hair. In the palms of its sweaty hands, the tod-
dler toys with the clump, soon fashioning it into a ball and
tossing it into the air, catching it with delight. The child
keeps tugging at the wool ball, pulling and twisting at it until
a soft string appears. Yarn. At bedtime, the mother finds the
string tucked under the child's reed sleeping mat. She has
never seen anything like it. She knows that she can turn
grasses into string and string into clothing. Yet new evidence
has just appeared — an unknown kind of string that she has
never before seen or realized possible — string from animal
hair. Cognitive dissonance.

I wake Evan early the next morning so that he can finish
his homework. He's still more interested in his knitting,
though. "Mom," he says fingering his uneven work, "this is
going to be a scarf." When I get him to the kitchen table for
breakfast and homework, he says, "I know my tradition,
Mom. I grow pumpkins every year for Halloween. That's my
tradition."

I smile inwardly, and tension in my belly loosens. When
we offer acceptance and patience, life rewards us by knitting
itself.

Jarmo

"Sorry, I'm not very focused," says Shirlee, one of my grant-writing clients. Shirlee is a respected Lakota elder in the Twin Cities American Indian community. The Lakota are the western branch of Minnesota's Dakota tribe, with whom they share a similar language. Though she was born on the Pine Ridge Indian Reservation in South Dakota, Shirlee has lived in the Twin Cities since the 1970s. You wouldn't know by looking at her that she is an elder. She has never let her hair go gray. With straight, shoulder-length dark brown hair, night-black eyes, high cheekbones, and always just a perfect touch of lipstick, Shirlee is gorgeous.

We are in the middle of a meeting. Our goal is to come up with a plan to raise money for City Indians, an upcoming exhibition for the not-for-profit art gallery that she founded in Minneapolis. Shirlee turns away from the whiteboard where she is listing potential funders for the exhibition and announces, "My grandson has been called up. He's leaving for Iraq soon."

I'm not sure what to say, so neither one of us says anything for a while. Shirlee rearranges a handful of colored dry-erase markers, until I break the silence. "I'm so sorry. When does he leave?"

"We don't know exactly when, but it's going to be soon," she answers. "Very soon. The only good news is that because he's such a good marksman, he'll be positioned at the rear of his company. I don't know where he learned to shoot. He never had a gun or went hunting when he was growing up. It must be the Lakota warrior blood in him." Shirlee laughs suddenly. Just as suddenly, her dark eyes cloud over and she continues in a near whisper. "They're going to send him to the north, where things are really dangerous, Nora."

History has been made in Iraq before. The oldest known village where humans domesticated animals in the West is the village of Jarmo. Jarmo sits in the mountains of northern Iraq, not far from the modern city of Kirkuk, which is the center of northern Iraq's petroleum industry, and not far from where Shirlee's grandson will be stationed. Archaeological evidence from around 7000 BCE shows that the people of Jarmo raised sheep in their fields, for food and to produce wool for the first time in recorded history.

The wool that the women of Jarmo spun and wove to turn into cloth offered many advantages over vegetable fibers like flax. Wool is a wonder fiber. It insulates against heat and cold, it absorbs and repels moisture, it resists fire, it's stretchy but not too stretchy, it's durable, it resists dirt, and it takes dyes quite easily. Who wouldn't want to wear wool, especially if you live in the north country like our family does? Except for outerwear — for which synthetics like Polarfleece have made a huge difference in how dry we can stay outside — my family's clothes come from much the same sources that clothed the families back in Jarmo.

The people of Jarmo belonged to the ancient world of

Mesopotamia — often labeled in Western history classes as the cradle of civilization. Wedged between the Tigris and Euphrates rivers, Mesopotamia was home to a handful of important cultures, including Sumeria and Babylonia. The Sumerian creation myth, the Enuma Elish, parallels the Dakota creation story. In the Enuma Elish, salt water and fresh water merge to form the earth.

I imagine that when the women of Jarmo woke up in the mornings to spin their wool into yarn, they saw evidence of creation in their everyday lives. Like the joining of the salt water and the fresh water, survival required bringing different elements together to create new life. To make children, they joined their bodies with those of their husbands. To grow food in their gardens, they added water from the sky to the roots below the ground. To make yarn, they took two strands of string spun from sheep's wool and twisted them together to form a single piece of a new, stronger string.

In English, the original meaning of the verb *knit* was to "draw close." When I return home from my meeting with Shirlee, I pull out Evan's sleeve, knitting — or drawing close — my fears for Shirlee's grandson, for all the soldiers serving in Iraq, and for all the Iraqi families who must endure the battles under way. Evan's flame pattern takes on a different feel in the fading November afternoon light. I don't see the Samhain bonfire any longer. I see bombs bursting in air.

During World War II, American women knit socks and sweaters for the troops in Europe. Although a few groups knit socks for American soldiers in Iraq today, Shirlee's grandson and the thousands of others stationed there do not want hot, hand-knit wool sweaters. The cradle of civilization is no longer a fertile Eden; it is a desert. But clothing, or the lack of it, has always been critical to survival to the people in the land that lies between the Tigris and the Euphrates. It was there that humans are believed to have first begun the art of writing. In one of the oldest stories ever written, the Mesopotamian fertility goddess Ishtar teaches us that clothing is necessary for life. Her story goes like this.

One day Ishtar decides to visit her sister in the underworld. She doesn't get a warm welcome. The sister strips Ishtar of all her clothes, layer by layer. She removes Ishtar's jewels, her cloak, and her dress. Naked, Ishtar is then put to death. Her passing devastates life in the Mesopotamian world. As Ishtar's lover tells the king of the Upper World:

> Since Ishtar has gone down to the Land of No Return,
> The bull springs not upon the cow,
> the ass impregnates not the jenny,
> In the street the man impregnates not the maiden.
> The man lay down in his own chamber,
> The maiden lay down on her side.[1]

Realizing that the survival of his kingdom depends on Ishtar's return, the king devises a plan to bring her back. But to return, Ishtar must retrieve her clothes. Without them, Mesopotamia will lose its chance at survival. The king's plan works, and Ishtar returns home, fully clothed. Like any good story, Ishtar's story knit a lesson for her ancient audience. Ishtar's journey is a reminder that clothing begets life.

Ishtar's near death reminds us that the women of Kirkuk still carry on Ishtar's story, and that when we knit, we carry it on, too. I knit with the hope that this ancient fertility goddess can bring life back to Jarmo today.

---

1 "Descent of Ishtar to the Netherworld," in A. Speiser and George A. Barton, *Archeology and the Bible*, 7th ed. (Philadelphia: American Sunday School Union, 1937), 530.

Slippers

*M*id-November brings the first snowfall. It's a light dusting — less than an inch that stays on the ground for a week and melts when the temperature climbs back above 32 degrees. While it's on the ground, this celestial covering warms rather than chills us, especially when we start a fire in the living room. Over the next week, we remain upbeat, even after the snow melts and disappears. It's as if we're cleansed by its pioneer visit. We're ready for this transition to winter.

November marks another transition — my birthday. For years, from the time I was a child, self-doubt used to jump from the shadows and into the foreground on my birthday. Something shifted in my forties. Though perhaps I should dread adding another year to my age, I now look forward to celebrating my birthday. The universe seems to respond. This year, I'm treated to three parties. The day before my birthday, Shirlee and her colleagues surprise me with chocolate meringue treats from a nearby bakery and a three-part-harmony rendition of

"Happy Birthday." On the evening of my birthday, Diego and the boys organize a party. And the next weekend, my parents invite our whole family over for cake and ice cream.

At our house on the night of my birthday, the boys pull out a sack of presents they've collected from Target and the Mall of America — which, along with Garrison Keillor's imaginary Lake Wobegon, put Minnesota on the map of must-see tourist destinations. Among the hastily wrapped gifts, I discover a turquoise ring from Diego, a silver watch from the boys, a pair of leather gloves from Andrew, and bath salts from all three. This potpourri of goods made all over the world glistens on our kitchen table as another sprinkling of snow gleams outside our skinny house by the river.

The most curious present is a pair of blue slippers from Evan. They look like the kind a little girl would wear, fuzzy slippers fashioned from fake rabbit fur. I try them on and practically fall over. The soles are padded with foam so thick that I struggle to balance. Diego, Evan, and Andrew are all smiling at me under the glow of the electric lights, waiting for my approval. I thank them for their gifts and float around the kitchen to hug each one of them.

Knitting offers plenty of transition points that mark change, like a birthday. We can celebrate the end of a row or the end of a piece. Transitions in daily life are harder to pinpoint. Is it the snow or just the passage of time that accounts for the ease that the boys are feeling now at school? Does winter arrive in Minnesota with the first snow that greets us in November, then melts away, or with the winter solstice and Christmas?

Transitions in the economy are even harder to pinpoint, though with hindsight, we can see that the evidence was there all along. Slow, almost imperceptible, economic transitions in the mountain valleys and plains around Jarmo affect all of us who knit and wear clothes today. For five thousand years, women of the Near East continued to card wool, spin yarn, and weave clothes for their families. But by about 1900 BCE, according to the historian Elizabeth Wayland Barber, they had grown so proficient at these skills that they began turning their domestic art into an industry. Several villages grew into large urban centers. The art of domesticating sheep and spinning wool began to spread all across the region.

Women played an important role in the region's economic growth, controlling the textile industry from their homes. In their households, they oversaw every step of textile production, from caring for the animals to weaving to managing a stable of workers, including slaves. The merchant women hired their husbands and traveling middlemen to take their woven goods on the trade routes to Anatolia, in modern-day Turkey.

Women were also in charge of deciding how to spend the money they earned. They made enough to pay taxes, run their households, and buy raw materials to make more textiles. "Keep an eye on that fellow who hasn't paid up for the cloth I sent with him to Anatolia," writes one woman in a cuneiform letter dated around 1900 BCE.[2]

Things might have stayed this way for much longer if Greek traders on the other side of Turkey hadn't begun bringing home both the woolen cloth and the art of commercial weaving. By about 1500 BCE, the Greeks had turned weaving into a big business, controlled by men. For the first time in recorded history, making clothes was used to make a

---

2 Elizabeth Wayland Barber, *Women's Work: The First 20,000 Years* (New York: W. W. Norton, 1994), 164.

profit outside the home. Women were no longer the chief executive officers.

In Greece, men broke the industry up into distinct specialties to fill larger and larger orders for textiles. Instead of running a one-stop domestic shop, they employed combers, spinners, weavers, and tailors, who worked in separate households or proto-factories. The middlemen, not the women, sold the products for cash in their growing empire. Free Greek women had to stay at home with their slaves, doing whatever was assigned to them.

Marija Gimbutas describes a significant shift in religious practice that coincides with this economic shift. In the Greek pantheon, the male gods now outranked the goddesses. Athena was born out of Zeus's head. Hades raped Demeter. I wonder if the real reason that Penelope kept weaving and unweaving her tapestry wasn't to keep her suitors in Ithaka at bay during Odysseus's long absence but to protest the loss of her power at the loom.

Many elements of the mother goddess did remain intact in the Greek pantheon of gods and goddesses. Take Artemis, a goddess associated with birth and found in different forms all over prehistoric Europe. In Greek times, she appeared to women at the birth of their children. The medicinal herb mugwort, or artemisia, was given to women to open the cervix during labor. Artemis is also associated with deer, resonating with the old European female deer figurines whose antlers return every spring, signaling the power of birth and rebirth. Ancient Greece also saw connections between weaving, birthing, and the divine. In the northern Greek city of Thessaly, women presented Artemis with offerings of loom weights, spindle whorls, and miniature figurines squatting to give birth.

If the independent, moneymaking women of Jarmo had known what would happen to their textiles and the goddess, would they have made different choices? Would they have stopped sending their woven goods up the trade routes to Turkey, or imposed tariffs on weaving imported from Greece? It's not human nature to give up power. Maybe they didn't realize what power they had had. Surely they didn't know that once they let it go, their art would be used to turn a larger profit. If the signs had been visible along the trade routes from Jarmo to Turkey, I think the women would have protected their household weaving industry. But they couldn't have protected what they didn't recognize as irreplaceable until it was too late.

Evan's sleeve feels a little like a kind of transition that won't be fully appreciated until some later date. Every evening I face my demon, the flame pattern. The transition from not-sleeve to sleeve is very subtle indeed. At this point, I have started and restarted the sleeve so many times that I've lost count. My fingers, brain, and yarn have not yet found the groove that will let me move beyond those first awkward rows of the flame pattern. Change is invisible here on my bamboo needles in November.

I forge ahead, thinking about the funny blue birthday slippers. I already have two pairs of slippers. Why would Evan pick out more slippers for me? And why fuzzy ones? Then I remember. The young helper at Abby's yarn shop wore fuzzy pink slippers. He was a boy, not a girl, and a knitter. Evan picked out a pair of blue slippers to complement Alex's slippers.

I hatch a plan. I will give Evan his sweater for Christmas. He knows about the sweater, of course — it was his idea. But he doesn't know *when* I will finish it. I will surprise him

Christmas morning with the completed sweater wrapped and under the tree. This possibility is what keeps me going — raveling and unraveling each twisted, messy row of goldenrod, maple-leaf red, and charcoal gray — for the next week.

I finish the first sleeve by Thanksgiving. It's a little lumpy. The flame pattern bulges out in the center like the crown of a snowbank. But I hold the finished sleeve up for the boys and Diego to admire. We all agree the ridge does look like a flame, not unlike the ones in the fire grate that warmed us after that first November snow.

Allah's Toes

I'm about to give up. The second sleeve is proving harder than the first one. I have ripped it out at least three times. First I was still leaving huge gaps in the knitting every time I switched from red to gold to gray. Then I discovered a better way to wrap the yarns together in the back each time I changed colors. But it took three tries before I figured that out.

Now, although I've mastered the art of wrapping the yarns in the back, I haven't figured out how to wrap them loosely enough. I've pulled the yarn so tight that there is no way the sleeve can hang straight. It looks like the cylindrical hunk of suet that Diego sets out for the birds as the temperature drops below zero outside. Rip for the third time; hello, sleeve attempt number four. Now I'm not sure I have the patience to start again. On the other hand, I'm so angry that I want to prove to myself that I can do it. But can I? It seems I've run into a crisis of faith here in the middle of Evan's second sweater sleeve.

My faith may seem tangential to Evan's sweater, but I want to testify that it's not. For two reasons. First, when we get into these ruts with our knitting, and everything, absolutely everything, is going wrong, we need faith. Faith that if we pull it out one more time, and even one more time after that, we will eventually figure it out. I must call on this kind of faith when I cast on the stitches for Evan's second sleeve yet again.

Second, the world's oldest known knitting artifact is literally an article of faith. It is a sock whose creator carefully knit the word *Allah* into the toe. Today it lives in the Textile Museum in Washington, DC.

Knitting arrived late on the scene in the world of women's textiles. Recent archaeological evidence from China suggests that knitting may have evolved in mainland Asia about five thousand years ago. That said, researchers aren't sure whether the Asian fabrics were examples of knitting or naalbinding — a related form of twisting string to form cloth. The sock dedicated to Allah was knit around the twelfth century CE in Egypt. This sock arrived about twenty thousand years after the first weaving and string skirts were made in Europe, and eight thousand years after wool was introduced in Mesopotamia.

According to a contemporary knitter named Lilinah biti-Anat, the Egyptian knitters used two-ply cotton and wool. Archaeological knitting remains from Egypt are found in many colors — indigo blue, red, golden yellow, cream yellow, green, salmon pink, turquoise, brown, and white. Not only did these pioneer Egyptian knitters have a lot of colors to choose from, but they also incorporated many colors into a single piece. Most of the knitted Egyptian fragments have at least three colors, and the woolen remains are knit in patterns of six colors or more. Evan's sleeve, with its three colors, seems simple by comparison.

Lilinah biti-Anat challenged herself to re-create the Egyptian sock of faith. It wasn't an easy task. The sock, originally knit in indigo blue and white cotton, has complex geometric and decorative patterns. It is composed of distinct sections, each one knit with its own unique abstract pattern. I see a section of flowers, a section of diamonds, a section of waves, and a section that looks like a constellation of stars in the night sky. And, of course, there's the toe section, with *Allah* knit into it.

I imagine what it might feel like to knit an object of devotion like this sock — both for Lilinah and for her knitting predecessor of a thousand years ago. I imagine all the fussing and careful work that goes into weaving the two colors evenly in and out of each round. I know because whenever I knit with two colors, I have to straddle the two challenges of not twining the different colored yarns too tightly, which leaves a puckered front side, or too loosely, which leaves gaps. But the Egyptian sock that Lilinah biti-Anat has re-created is perfectly smooth and whole. What is harder for me to imagine is what it would feel like to wear these special socks. Would they be a reminder that each step of the way is made with Allah as the guide?

Evan's gift of the blue slippers now feels especially appropriate. I should walk with care and precision each literal step of the way as I fashion his sweater.

There is a labyrinth mown in the grass lawn at the Catholic women's college half a mile from our house, down the Randolph hill. This labyrinth exactly replicates the one at Chartres Cathedral in France. Faithful pilgrims enter the maze and follow it back and forth into the center of the circle and out again, a path that winds three-quarters of a mile inside a small circle. When Diego and I walked it last spring, he said, "You never know which direction you're headed."

"But you know you're being guided every step of the way," I replied.

The medieval Egyptian socks are like a portable labyrinth, with a divinity guiding the foot no matter where you go — to the mosque, to the marketplace, to the library, or back home. Allah follows you; or, rather, you follow Allah.

Each step of the way, I think. In knitting, we move step by step, too. There are no shortcuts. Every stitch is an act unto itself. And without one stitch completed, you cannot move on to the next one.

I start up the sleeve again. To finish this sleeve, I must tumble a bit farther down Alice's rabbit hole. Here in the darkness, I discover faith. Not big, earth-quaking faith, but the quiet, graceful faith that comes with knitting one stitch at a time.

Pob Pov

*E*van comes home from school this week with a large cardboard figure of a Hmong boy wearing a traditional outfit: black pants, black jacket, and black hat with a red pompom on top. The Hmong New Year celebration will take place next weekend in downtown St. Paul, and tens of thousands from St. Paul and around the country will attend. We admire Evan's work, and then he asks, "Mom, can we knit again?"

"After dinner," I say.

When we do sit down to knit, I follow my two guides — Abby's notes and the adult sweater pattern. It's finally getting a little easier, though I am forced to stick my tongue out in concentration like a little kid. I admire the brilliant goldenrod gold and maple-leaf red that are beginning to march up Evan's second sleeve, their boldness contrasting vividly with the charcoal background.

Evan's colors would appeal to my Hmong colleague Pa Dee, who once observed that so many Americans like bland colors: lots of tans, whites, browns, and blacks. When our fledgling Hmong organization was getting under way, a public relations firm offered to design our logo. I went with Pa Dee and the organization director to a brainstorming meeting in the PR company offices. I remember sitting in the black and silver boardroom feeling doubtful they would be able to understand the recent Hmong experience of war and immigration. Our director did most of the talking, emphasizing that the partnership concept behind our name — Hmong American Partnership — should leap out of the logo.

Then Pa Dee blurted out, "Please use bright colors. When Hmong people stitch story cloths for Americans, they tone down the colors — using boring grays and tans and browns and dark blues to go with American decor. But back in Laos or when we sew for ourselves, we use lots of bright colors. Red, for example, is used in our baby carriers to keep away evil spirits. Bright pink and bright green are two of our most traditional colors."

The PR team listened. When we returned a few weeks later, they unveiled a logo that looked like two hot pink hands wrapped around the agency's named spelled out in a fluorescent lime green. Pa Dee loved it. It turns out, though, that she wasn't 100 percent historically accurate about the colors.

Hmong embroidery has employed bright colors during all of Pa Dee's life. But, according to Hmong elders, their textiles didn't become brightly colored until after the Hmong began working for the U.S. government in the 1960s to help defeat the North Vietnamese. Before the war, Hmong families were busy working in the fields year-round. They lived high in the mountains, far from the towns or cities where Chinese merchants sold brightly colored threads. When they did travel to town, they had to go on foot, taking days to reach a big market. Women used plants from the mountains to dye their embroidery thread. The color choices were limited.

After the war began, Hmong men began earning surplus cash that could be used to purchase goods in the town markets. As the war escalated, many Hmong families sought safety from the heavy bombing by moving out of the remote mountains and closer to the market towns and an American air base in Laos. The newfound cash and proximity to larger markets gave Hmong women access to imported, multicolored Chinese thread for their hand-crafted textiles.

Though access to colors has changed over time, the needlework of the Hmong remains distinctive. Hmong textile artists combine cross-stitch, appliqué, reverse appliqué, and embroidery into decorative squares called *paj ntaub*. Pronounced "pah en-dow," *paj ntaub* means "flower cloths" in English. Traditionally, Hmong girls learned all four of these sewing techniques from their mothers, just as European American girls in the preindustrial United States used to sew samplers, beginning with the ABCs at age five and graduating to elaborate pictorials that showed off their embroidery skills.

While American girls tended to stick to representational images, Hmong girls learned how to sew the traditional Hmong symbols for mountains, snails, elephants, and dragons. Under periods of Chinese repression, Hmong writing was outlawed. The Hmong used these *paj ntaub* symbols to replace their alphabet when exchanging messages between villages. Though the meaning of the symbols is now lost, the method of stitching and the use of vibrant color and bold traditional designs survive.

Unlike the old American samplers, which used to be

framed, the Hmong *paj ntaub* is put to use. Each *paj ntaub* square is sewn onto everyday clothes or ritual dress, like the clothes the Hmong wear to the New Year's celebration. The Hmong New Year begins on the weekend closest to the first day of the waxing moon of the twelfth month of the year, at the first cock's crow — around three in the morning. In St. Paul the celebration is generally celebrated on the first full weekend in November. Like the Irish, the Hmong honor the spirits of their ancestors at this time of year.

A secondary reason for the celebration is to bring together young unmarried men and women. It's no surprise, then, that at New Year's everyone wears their finest clothes — the very best Sunday best. Women show off their embroidery skills by wearing colorful *paj ntaub* sewn onto the edge of their skirts and on the backs of their blouses. They also wear a traditional small rectangular apron called a *sev*, which is pronounced "shay." Until the Hmong involvement in the Vietnam War, the *sev* was sewn in simple black. Women tied it, like an apron, over the front of their skirts. Today Hmong women wear the brightest and boldest of colors and patterns to the Hmong New Year's in St. Paul: hot pink beaded hats, brightly stitched leggings, ornate silver jewelry, and intricately stitched aprons, or *sev*, decorated with colorful *paj ntaub*.

To get the courtship ball rolling, literally, the young men and women are paired up, facing each other in two straight lines — women in one line, men facing them. Each pair tosses a ball back and forth in a game called *pob pov*. In the old days, the ball was made of cloth. Today in St. Paul, it's a lime-green tennis ball. If you drop the ball, you have to pay a forfeit to your partner. Options include singing a song, telling a story, or giving them something — even an article of clothing that you're wearing.

At bedtime, I wrap up my fledgling flamed sleeve, and Evan reluctantly goes up the stairs to brush his teeth. I follow him, stopping at the landing in front of the Hmong story cloth my colleagues gave me in 1995. This one is filled with brightly embroidered animals in a forest. Pink birds, golden elephants, and purple tigers share a paradise of peace and harmony. Color, lots of color.

All of a sudden the realization hits me like a blaze as bright as the flame in Evan's sleeves. The ancient European string skirt is alive and well right here in St. Paul. The Hmong *sev* is a cousin to the ritual string skirts worn by the Venus figurine in France and by the women worshipping in the goddess temples across ancient Europe. The temples and the Venus figures are gone, but the Hmong have preserved their cloth apron for thousands of years, bringing it from northern China to southern China, from China to Laos, from Laos to Minnesota.

For the Hmong, New Year's is the time of year for regeneration. The harvest is in. The cycle of life must start anew. In this dark season, the bright colors and bold designs in the young women's *sev* help the couples catch not only the ball but also each other.

Needles

$\mathcal{I}$ return to the second of Evan's two sleeves with a new enthusiasm mixed with a lot of awe. I'm not only a mom knitting a sweater for her son in a skinny blue house by the Mississippi River in the American Midwest. I am also a member of a craft whose history is alive and well right here in my community and in this country. This isn't a distant or impersonal history. Our Hmong friends, neighbors, teachers, and classmates are heirs to the ancient traditions of women weaving and wearing ritual skirts to regenerate the community. I'm not Hmong, nor do I wear a string skirt, but I revere this continuous chain of clothing. Though knitting, perhaps only a thousand years old, is one of the newest forms of textile creation, today's knitters are also a part of this ancient textile history — even a novice knitter like me, struggling to knit a sweater for my son by Christmas.

Soon my reverence and awe begin to dissipate. I've made it past the second flame only to discover a new challenge. At the end and at the beginning of each row I'm directed to add stitches. These increases will make the sleeve wide enough to go around the upper arms. But the extra stitches bunch up and want to fall off my double-pointed bamboo needles. I try not to complain too much. I like bamboo needles. They're smoother than the metal needles I grew up learning to knit on, and they don't make that constant clicking noise that metal ones do. But my bamboo needles aren't long enough to hold all the stitches in place, so I'm yearning after the louder, old-fashioned ones. It's a double-edged sword.

Knitters have invented many different kinds of needles, also known as pricks, wires, and pins over the years. Archaeological evidence indicates that the first knitters in North Africa relied on knitting wires made from brass. Across the Mediterranean in Europe, knitters used a variety of materials to make needles, from ivory, boxwood, and whalebone to an increasingly accessible metal, steel. The original cottage-industry knitters in England commissioned their local blacksmiths to make their steel needles at the forge. In New Zealand, rural knitters made needles out of fencing wire.

Knitters across time have also varied the shape and style of needles they use. Some knitters used knitting sticks, which they used to hold their needles in place and speed up their work. Photographs of old Cornish knitting sticks evidence hefty needles that look more like the hilt of a sword than a delicate knitting device. The carvers, often men, engraved whorls and diamonds and patterns almost as elaborate as on the knitted guernseys and jerseys. It is said that a hopeful admirer of a knitter would carve a knitting stick or two for his intended bride — whittling in designs with special meanings, or perhaps his beloved's name.

Until about the time that sweaters moved inland from the fishing ports of Great Britain, most knitters in Europe worked in the round on at least four needles. In Turkey, knitters also worked in the round, but on five needles. Knitting flat separate pieces on just two needles came into fashion after the Industrial Revolution, when people demanded flatter-looking clothing produced by the machine-powered looms.

The shift to two needles brought other changes. Until the late 1800s, women tended to hold their knitting by holding the needles with their thumbs and palms upward. That's how I still hold my needles, by the way. But in fashion parlors and salons around France and England, women began to hold their needles like a pen or pencil. They'd hold on to the tip of each needle with their thumb and forefinger, palms down. The result? Their dainty hands and bejeweled fingers were more easily admired by the men, or, I suppose, potential mothers-in-law, in the drawing rooms of Paris and London. Some knitters argue this style wasn't just about looks and have adopted it into today's knitting circles. But when I try this method out on Evan's sweater, I find it impossible to keep control of the yarn or to keep sufficient tension in each stitch I take. In fact, this method leads me further and further away from the lesson of the Egyptian sock of faith — remember to make each stitch count.

Today knitters can choose from dozens of different kinds of knitting needles to buy. We don't need to go down to the local blacksmith to commission a pair of "points." Instead, we can order needles online or visit our favorite local yarn shop.

I've counted at least eight different kinds of knitting needles readily available in the contemporary American knitting market. There are glass needles that have rainbow-colored, hand-blown tips. There are plastic-coated Pony Pearl needles that make for a very fast knit. There are Bryspun needles, also plastic, that claim to be easy on the hands of those with arthritis. There are casein (milk protein) needles that are said to be quieter than plastic or metal needles and very smooth. There are nickel needles and aluminum needles, which are both very fast and lightweight, though nickel needles are more expensive. There are needles made from woods of all kinds, from pine to ebony and rosewood.

Then there are my favorites, bamboo needles, which are very strong, like metal, but much quieter. They came highly recommended when I started my sock project last winter. More important, they worked. I made it through the socks, and when it came time to buy larger needles for Evan's sweater, I felt no desire to try any other kind. I trust my bamboo needles to get me through. They're safer than metal, too.

Though I learned to knit on metal needles as a child, I don't think I will ever use them again — not after hearing what happened to Paula Lalish in Washington State a few years ago. Paula, a longtime knitter, was knitting a sweater one August in the car while her husband was driving them home. All of a sudden they heard a sound like a shot ricocheting through their car. They thought they'd been hit by a gunman, or perhaps a hunter. Neither proved to be the case. Yet the sound was so loud that Paula's ears went on ringing for hours. The impact on her left hand was so strong that her index finger turned blue and began to swell. After Paula put ice on her finger, she and her husband discovered that her metal knitting needle had exploded. The aluminum-coated needles had been moving so fast in Paula's hands that a powder by-product in the needle had shot off like a bullet inside the car.[3]

I decide, however, to knit as fast as a shooting bullet, sticking firm to my double-pointed bamboo needles. I'm not as fast as Paula, but if I stay the course, I can see my way to the end of Evan's second sleeve. I force myself to sit back down in my comfy chair by the fireplace and finish the red flame streaking across the dark gray night.

---

3 Jan Halliday, "The Case of the Exploding Knitting Needle," *Port Townsend and Jefferson County Leader*, August 11, 2004, www.ptleader .com/print.asp?ArticleID=10138&SectionID=36&SubSectionID=55 (accessed September 9, 2008); and Paula Lalish, "The Case of the Exploding Knitting Needle," at www.paulalalish.com/needle.htm (accessed 10/29/08).

Thanksgiving

*B*oth sleeves are done. Hallelujah! I stretch them out to admire the work. All the effort recedes; front and center are the two flames. Each flame is mostly red, outlined in Evan's goldenrod three-quarters of the way up the arm. The golden tip curls around like a wisp of warm breath in cold air. I'm not sure how I ever managed to finish them, but the material evidence is about to go on display.

Evan wants to try on the pieces now. He bends over, and I set the back piece over his seven-year-old frame. Then I wrap the two sleeves over his outstretched arms. He parades around the living room modeling all three sweater pieces.

"See Mom, I'm flying," he says flapping both flames like wings and leaning forward so the back doesn't slip off.

"Wow," I say, wrapping the ends of the charcoal gray into a tidy ball. Evan takes this encouragement and pushes it a little further.

"Now I'm really flying," he repeats. This time he's standing on the edge of the couch and he jumps off onto the floor.

The three pieces fall off and land in a heap next to my chair. Evan lands on his bottom. Loudly.

"That was fun!" he says, pretending he's not feeling any pain.

I scoop the three pieces back up. Evan stands next to me as I fold them and set them on top of my knitting basket. I feel the warmth of his body next to mine and give him a hug — a hug that's big enough to hold all of our gratitude.

I'm feeling a lot of gratitude this season. It's Thanksgiving, after all. I know the story of the Pilgrims and the Indians has been reworked to suit the best interests of the American and British colonists. I know, too, that the Dakota only received one-hundredth of the amount they were owed for selling this land where we make our home — two thousand dollars, not the two hundred thousand they were promised. Still, I love my mother's huge turkey dinner with stuffing, mashed potatoes, gravy, cranberries, and, best of all, her pumpkin pie.

This Thanksgiving, we are breaking tradition and starting a few new ones of our own. Instead of making pie with canned pumpkin, Evan and I are going to make a pumpkin pie from the pumpkins he grew. Ever the individualist, Andrew doesn't like pumpkin pie. He pleads with me to make his favorite — key lime pie. I oblige. Making pies becomes a family affair. Diego has already scooped out the seeds and baked one of Evan's huge pumpkins in the oven. The resulting tawny mash and the pie crust dough that I made for both pies earlier in the day are chilling in the refrigerator. All we have to do is roll the crust and make the two fillings. For that we need Andrew. His job is to make wisecracks from the couch where he's reading.

Pumpkins belong to the squash family and are native to

the Americas. Through all the thousands of years that indigenous people grew, cooked, and ate pumpkins, it seems, they never turned food production into big business — agribusiness, as we call it now. Families and tribes grew as much as they could store in their cache pits for the long winter months. Evan and I measure out the cooked pumpkin and add milk, eggs, and spices. What ingredients are needed for a culture to turn survival into profit?

It seems a quirk of history that in some parts of the world an enterprise can remain largely unchanged for thousands of years — like women weaving woolen cloth in Mesopotamia, knitting socks in Egypt, or growing pumpkins in North America.

Sometimes a cultural tradition can even travel thousands of miles without changing, like the Hmong *sev*, the cloth cousin of the ancient European string skirt. Yet in other parts of the world, the exchange of goods leads to huge economic and cultural shifts. In Greece, weaving was transformed from a woman's household industry into a male-controlled, profit-making economic enterprise. Would it have been possible to predict the impact of exchanging goods on a day in late November in seventeenth-century America?

I don't think anyone imagined that a new empire would sprout up from the "new" land — one that would end up feeding the world with its grain by the beginning of the twentieth century, much of it shipped from Duluth, Minnesota, the world's largest inland port. The women of the Near East didn't choose to lose their household weaving industry some two thousand years ago. Nor do I think that the indigenous people of the Americas would have taught the colonialists how to plant corn, beans, and squash in the 1600s if they'd known they'd lose their land.

Both pies come out of the oven without alarm. Evan's pie is a perfect golden brown. Andrew's lime custard is a little wiggly, but the tart aroma is wonderful. We are ready to go over the river to Grandmother's house — literally. My parents live ten minutes by car across the Mississippi. When we cross the river, I look off to my right. There is Pike Island, the ancestral home of the Dakota Indian people. I look down at the keychain that my Ojibwe friend Betty beaded for me when I turned forty. It is full of Betty's good-heartedness. I start singing, "Over the river and through the woods, to Grandmother's house we go!" The boys join in, and then Diego. But everyone protests because his singing voice wobbles in all the wrong places. Before we know it, we're seated at my mother's long table and eating everything, including the pumpkin pie.

Back at home, I drop off to sleep with thanksgiving in my heart and in my belly. I am grateful for the chance to be with my family. I am grateful for my children and for my dearest Diego. I am grateful for my friends. I am grateful, too, for the countless women who over history have formed a chain linking us all the way back to the first knitters in Egypt, the cloth makers in ancient Iraq, the traveling Hmong *sev* makers, and the flax weavers in Moravia and Ukraine. I am grateful that Evan's two flamed sleeves are finally done.

The Front

DECEMBER

At Rest

*K*nitting is the only thing that I'm not doing now that I've finished the sleeves for Evan's sweater. I should get started on the front, but there's nearly a whole month until my Christmas deadline. I'm cocky — like someone who's been on a diet for a few weeks, loses a few pounds, and decides to eat a brownie, or two. Here's a more generous attitude: I'm giving myself a period of rest. In her book *Journal of a Solitude*, the poet May Sarton writes, "The most valuable thing we can do for the psyche, occasionally, is to let it rest, wander, live in the changing light of a room, not try to be or do anything."[1]

"Changing light of a room" doesn't ring true for Minnesotans this time of year. We are just a few weeks away from the winter solstice, the shortest day of the year. Here in the northland, we observe the changing *darkness* in a room.

---

1 May Sarton, *Journal of a Solitude* (New York: W. W. Norton, 1973; reprint, 1992), 89.

Shadows linger in the living room until 9:30 in the morning, returning again by four o'clock. In this changing darkness, I lose a friend. Four weeks ago, an aneurysm erupted in Tania's brain. She went into a coma and never came out. Like Evan's sweater, Tania's life is unfinished. There is no front, no final seam that knits together her life. Tonight Diego and I will attend her memorial service at the university where she taught — halfway between Borealis Yarns and the compost site where I dropped off our fall leaves just seven weeks ago.

Tania moved to Minnesota from Israel less than two years ago, yet I felt like I'd known her for years. Like me, she was recently divorced and wanted to create a safe space for her sons, ages ten and twelve. We shared our stories about hiding our hearts to survive in our first marriages. We both knew what it felt like to stow away the spirit in order to survive. We were both relearning how to bring this spirit back into our lives. The last time I saw Tania, we walked to the river and back. It was the very end of August, hot and humid, so unlike now, the cold and dark near the winter solstice. Beds of orange tiger lilies waved. Thick hostas, bearing long shoots of purple flowers, flirted with their unopened buds. Crowns of aster and goldenrod sang out on every block. We talked and walked so fast and hard it felt like the wind was pulling us in two directions — down to the river and back up again. Then school started, for our boys and for Tania. Three months, and then at the end of November a mutual friend called to tell me about the brain damage, the coma. She called again to tell me of Tania's death and the ceremony scheduled for tonight.

Tania is the third friend I've lost. A friend from Woodward Court died in my second year of college, and in my thirties, I lost a colleague from the Minneapolis American Indian

Center who had moved back home to the Pine Ridge Indian Reservation in South Dakota. I didn't make it to my college friend's funeral, but several of us from work drove out across the plains and into the Badlands for Terri's funeral. After the mass, we walked into the community room and found a long line of folding tables covered in photographs and cards wishing Terri well on her journey into the spirit world. Dozens of multicolored star quilts also hung over the tables and on the wall behind, forming a galaxy of appreciation for this powerful woman who, like Tania, was taken away while she was still young.

Quilting is a textile tradition long practiced in the African American community, too. During the time of slavery, quilts were encoded with the itinerary for the Underground Railroad that would lead to safety in the North — not unlike the stitched embroidery symbols the Hmong used to send messages between clans and regions to protect their clans from the Chinese. African American textiles, however, long predate the period of enslavement in this country.

Because the oldest human remains have been found in Africa, it's likely that this continent is home to the longest tradition of textile making in the world. However, the warm climate has worked against preserving ancient cloth remains. The oldest cloth found in Africa, in the Igbo region of today's Nigeria, dates only to the ninth century. Yet today Africa contains examples of almost every kind of textile production known to humans. From knitting traditions in Egypt in the north to beadwork among the Xhosa and Zulu in the south, Africa celebrates the art of decorated cloth in every corner of the continent. These textile traditions burst from the land like shooting stars full of light and power, so unlike the darkness in the northland this season.

Many African cloth-making traditions also reverberate with the connections between women's powers and textiles found in the Middle East, in Europe, and among the Hmong. Or perhaps it is the other way around — that cloth making around the world carries the echoes of Africa. Sometimes the threads that connect us across continents are so old or fragile that they become invisible, like a friend who has been taken from life.

A more visible thread is the one that connects African American quilt makers with the textile artists of West Africa. In Sierra Leone and Liberia, for example, weavers create colorful strips of cloth anywhere from one to eighteen inches wide. When the required number of strips have been prepared, the weavers sew them together to form bold geometric mazes. Surely African American quilters hold in their hands ancestral knowledge of piecing together small strips of cloth to make a powerful whole.

Many African textiles connote the power of women, too. The Kalabari people, who originated in the Niger Delta region of West Africa, make reverse appliqué cloth, or *pelete bite*, which honors the powers of the great mythical mother, Owamekaso. Indeed, the cut-thread designs in the Kalabari cloth often contain bountiful images of mothers and children, reminiscent of Ishtar's fertility powers in ancient Iraq. Among the Yoruba people of West Africa, a special kind of cloth called *adire* contains magic. Women traditionally print resist designs onto the cloth using cassava-flour paste, then dye it in a rich indigo blue dye. According to Norma Wolff, the Yoruba women call upon Iya Mapo, the female protector of cloth, while they are dyeing *adire* cloth:

Iya Mapo, mother of mothers,
calm old mother of the earth,

on the day we came down to earth
From heaven
You gave us our profession.
Your provide for us
Better than the market.
You provide for us better than the farm.[2]

By calling Iya Mapo in song, the women invoke this ancient mother's protection for the dye and the cloth — and for the wearers of this sacred Yoruba cloth.

In central Africa, the Kuba people embroider tapestries using raffia thread. The largest articles are embroidered dance skirts called *nchak*. They are adorned with sewn or cut-out abstract designs and symbols whose meanings have been lost. Yet the dance skirt is a familiar piece. Perhaps the Kuba's ancestors danced dances of fertility as ancient European women did or engaged in community rituals of regeneration like *pob pov*, as the Hmong still do today.

Other cloths in Africa that link cloth to the power of women include *bogolanfini*, which the Mande people make in Mali. This cloth, dyed with natural fibers and mud, is worn to honor major transitions in life, including birth, marriage, and death. In Tunisia, a bride traditionally wears seven layered tunics for her wedding, a celebration that lasts for several days. On the seventh day, the bride takes off an embroidered belt. She puts the belt back on after the groom has entered her and keeps it for the rest of her life. It is especially important during childbirth, when she ties it to the wall

---

2 Quoted in Norma Wolff, "'Leave Velvet Alone': The Adire Tradition of the Yoruba," in *Cloth Is the Center of the World: Nigerian Textiles, Global Perspectives*, ed. Susan J. Torntore (Minnesota: Goldstein Museum of Design, 2001), 57–58.

and pulls on it, linking the mother-to-be to the important
Muslim figure Fatima, daughter of Muhammad and mother
of Hassan and Hussein. Like Fatima, my two friends Tania
and Terri were mothers to sons, who now must make their
way without their birth mothers.

As Diego and I drive back home from Tania's memorial
service, a light snow falls. Each snowflake drops with the
weight of my sorrow. I want to be able to call Tania up and
take another walk to the river. I want to tell her how I'm
fighting my demon self-doubt and catch up on how she's
fighting her demons. I want to show her the sweater I'm knitting for Evan. These desires, and the knowledge that they
can't be met, swell inside me. Anger ricochets around my
body in a battle that can't be won. Like Evan's sweater, Tania's
life is unfinished. The back to Evan's sweater is like Tania's
childhood — the skeleton on which a life, a body rests. The
two sleeves are like Tania's two boys — the flames of energy
and life that emerged from her body. But there is no front, no
final seam that knits together her life.

In this dark season, I wish Tania's two sons could grab a
magical woven belt from Tunisia to link them back to their
mother. I wish for them a patchwork quilt that will guide
them to their mother like those once used on the Underground Railroad to journey north to safety. I wish for them a
star quilt that shines so brightly they can find their mother in
the galaxy of stars that protects us night after night, even in
this darkest time of the year.

Dropped Stitches

I have a confession to make: I drop stitches. I can be working along in the simplest of patterns, like stockinette. Knit one row, purl the next. I get going so fluidly that I no longer have to look down to guide the yarn. Sometimes the needles start moving fast enough that I hear the sound of the bamboo sticks beating together like a soft drum. It's no longer me knitting — the mom in the skinny blue house by the river. My hands and my volition are no longer in the equation. Knitting is simply happening.

Then something pulls me out of this steady rhythm. The phone rings. Evan asks me to look at his latest paper-airplane design. Andrew comes downstairs for a bowl of cereal. In the split second that I look up, the magical movement of the knitting needles is gone. I'm back, sitting in my chair by the fireplace, with all my responsibilities and daily duties. Doubts arise again in my mind. Am I doing a good enough job — with my kids, with my grant writing, with my knitting?

A quick review of any day yields all the evidence I need

to prove that I drop metaphorical stitches, too. This morning, Andrew and I were in the kitchen playing a game of Rummy 500 — not just for leisure, but to keep us both awake until he had to leave for school.

"Mom, I'm still cold," Andrew whimpers.

"Put your sweatshirt on — the one Aunt Cate gave you," I say, discarding the jack of hearts.

"Okay, but I was cold all night long. I'll never warm up," he says, laying down the three of spades.

After he leaves, I go upstairs and investigate Andrew's bedroom. The room is tiny, only twelve by seven feet. This summer I encouraged the boys to turn their beds ninety degrees — away from the longer wall and under the window. Evan refused, but Andrew obliged. His bed now stretches horizontally under his window. What was a welcome breeze in the hot, humid summer has turned into a polar chill for the poor kid. No wonder he was cold this morning. Not only is his bed in the wrong place, but he doesn't have enough coverings. He's got a set of blue jersey sheets and a single navy blue blanket because of his allergies. The doctors told us he should never sleep with a thick comforter because it would attract dust mites. Now that it's December, the single blue blanket isn't enough.

I dropped a stitch.

I go downstairs to the basement and open an old wicker basket I inherited from my grandmother, where I keep a small collection of textiles. I've got a few batik sarongs from Java — my favorite has maroon sea creatures and fish swimming in an indigo blue sea. I've got a Balinese double ikat runner, handmade, the patterns formed by dyeing both the warp and the weft. I've got an old bolt of paisley cotton, from a fabric store in Boston, that once served as curtains. I've got a long green machine-woven sari from Nepal. And I've got a red Mexican blanket.

The Mexican blanket reminds me of other dropped stitches. So far my research into textiles has yielded information about the history of weaving and knitting in Europe, Africa, the Middle East, and parts of Asia. What about women in the Americas? Surely women made clothes for their families here, too? I only have my gut to follow. That and this red blanket sitting in my grandmother's wicker basket.

After Bob Dylan left Minneapolis in the early 1970s, hippies still sold goods and played their guitars on street corners all around the University of Minnesota campus near the river and my high school. One of the prime spots was on the Washington Avenue Bridge, because when it got cold, the vendors and musicians could move their wares into the covered pedestrian walkway. Another popular place to set up shop was on the sidewalk between Gray's Drug and Ragstock, the shop where I purchased my favorite striped sweater. I liked browsing the jewelry, candles, bongs, and tie-dyed shirts for sale. But I didn't buy anything from the hippie vendors until my senior year of high school, when a new shop opened up on the second floor of Gray's Drug, called Maya Market.

Maya Market sold goods from Mexico and countries farther south. When it was warm, the shop owner would peddle his wares outside. One day I spied a red striped Mexican cotton blanket. It sat on the sidewalk, folded neatly among the parking meters with a dozen other blankets and huarache leather sandals. I wanted it. Like my striped sweater, this blanket followed me to Chicago for college. Though I lost track of my sweater, the blanket is right here in my wicker textile basket, in a skinny blue house by the river.

It turns out that weaving is as well established in the Americas as it is in Europe, Africa, Asia, and Mesopotamia. Two of the four original cotton species in the world are indigenous to the Americas — or Ixachilanka, as the entire continent, both North and South America, is called in the Nahuatl language. One cotton is native to Mexico; the second cotton is native to the Pacific coast of Chile and Peru. Some elders say that the cotton from Mexico once came in four colors, though today it grows almost entirely in white. Clothing was critical to survival in Ixachilanka, both for individuals and for the culture.

Before the Spanish colonialists invaded Mexico, the clothes people wore indicated the level of respect they had earned from the community. For example, no matter the family's circumstances, anyone could become a warrior. The warriors protected themselves in battle with thickly padded cotton armor. After battle, a man could earn, or lose, the right to wear better clothes. One writer observed: "He who does not dare go to war from now on will be deprived. . . . He will have to wear the (maguey) clothing of the common man. And in this way his cowardice, his weak heart will be known by all. He will not wear cotton garments. He will not wear feathers, he will not receive flowers like the great Lords."[3]

Women in ancient Mexico wore skirts — the longer, the better. According to one Mexican elder, when a woman's skirt touches the ground, she can channel the earth's energy to her female reproductive organs. Women also wore woven belts around their abdomens that retained heat and supported their

---

3 Patricia Rieff Anwalt, *Indian Clothing before Cortés: Mesoamerican Costumes from the Codices* (Norman: University of Oklahoma Press, 1981), 28.

internal organs. The complexity of the design, as well as the material used to make the clothing, revealed a woman's status and level of knowledge. Young women wore plain skirts made of maguey, a plant with low, thick leaves also known as agave. As they aged, progressing in their knowledge, wisdom, and merit, women could add wide borders designed with many different colors, motifs, and feathers.

The Mexihca, or precontact indigenous people of the lands we call Mexico, made an annual offering of woven cloth to their leaders. To symbolize women's ties to the loom, every girl was given a spindle at birth. Girls began by weaving coarse vegetable fibers like maguey for their own families. As they grew older, they wove cotton as fine as silk for the annual offering. Like the Mesopotamians and the Greeks, the Mexihca threaded textiles into their mythology.

Spirit beings, or unseen energies sometimes called gods or goddesses, did not live in separate spheres of existence in the ancient world of Ixachilanka, according to my friend Deborah, originally from El Paso, Texas, and a student of Mexihca culture. These earthly spirits represent different aspects of the trials and joys of human existence and of the elements. To learn how to live in greater harmony with the universe, humans study the life stories and experiences of the spirits and their cosmic energies.

One such energy in the Mexihca cosmos is a feminine entity named Tlazolteotl. Her name is pronounced "te-lah-sohl-TEY-oat." Tlazolteotl is known as the lady of cotton and regeneration. Like Iya Mapo among the Yoruba, Ishtar in Mesopotamia, and Artemis in Greece, she is a great mother. She spins together the black earth and the red wisdom of the ancients, creating a balance in the universe that aids women in childbirth. She gives fertility to the fields by recycling and renewing nutrients in the soil. The line drawings from the ancient codices and in archaeological finds illustrate her powers. Tlazolteotl wears a flowing cotton headdress. Two spools of cotton hang from her ears. She is almost always shown giving birth to a child out of the belly of her long, highly decorated skirt.

Tlazolteotl is honored especially during the end of winter, when the energy of the earth is renewed and the fields will soon be ready for planting. That is, she pulls energy from the dark season and the resting soil so that the community can renew itself. It is no surprise, then, that she is also the protector of the ceremonial sweat lodge, or *temazcal*. This structure is built like a womb — low and covered, often made of adobe, where one enters the darkness for purification. After the ceremony, one emerges as if reborn.

Tlazolteotl conveys the importance of digging deep into the earth, gestating in the darkness for a while, and emerging with newfound wisdom. Cotton is the tool she uses to help humans understand this process of transformation and renewal. Tlazolteotl's wisdom is woven into the clothes the Mexihca wear for survival and for acknowledgment of human wisdom and the feminine power of regeneration.

The survival of a culture hangs in a delicate balance. Tlazolteotl shows us one way to find this balance — by not being afraid to go into the dark, into the deep. For when we risk this journey, we reemerge with new energy. Clothes and cotton — real or metaphorical — are the medium through which and from which human life can be born. Without them, humans will die.

Andrew needs an extra blanket to stay warm this winter. The red Mexican blanket is perfect. It's warm enough to protect my child, yet thin enough to throw into the washing machine every week. I lift the blanket out of the basket and carry it back up to Andrew's room. I spread it on top of his blue blanket, thinking of Tlazolteotl. She and this blanket are my reminder to remain wary of, yet attentive to, dropped stitches, in knitting, in history, and at home. They are my validation to keep digging into the darkness to see what I can cull for greater wisdom in this life.

Quipus

*A*fter a two-week period of rest and reflection, I have newfound energy for Evan's sweater. There are just two weeks till Christmas. I may be awake until long after Santa Claus shoots back up the chimney, but I'm determined to have the sweater wrapped under the Christmas tree. There's only the front piece left. I cast on and start the first few rows with ease. With no complicated flame pattern to incorporate, no twisting and turning of three colors, I can fly. I haven't dropped any stitches, yet.

Finishing Evan's sweater isn't the only task I need to accomplish before Christmas, of course. There's a tree to be bought, put up, and decorated. There are presents for the extended family, all in various stages of readiness — from already purchased and wrapped to nonexistent. I don't have a clue what to get either my father or Diego. There are cookies to bake and a Christmas Day meal to plan.

Grant writing does not let up during this period, either. One or two funders always have January 1 deadlines, which means that those of us on the asking end have to keep planning and writing. In the midst of all this activity, evidence of knitting in South America makes the front pages of the newspaper. The people of Bolivia elect Evo Morales as their president on December 18, 2005. This former llama herder from the high Andean plains is the first indigenous leader in South America since the Spanish conquest. His informal attire makes almost as much news as his victory. Like Evan, Morales was born in October. Apparently, they also both like sweaters.

Mr. Morales wears his trademark alpaca sweaters just about everywhere he goes: to visit heads of states and to talk to his constituents in the cities and in the high Andean communities where llamas (and coca) are still central to the indigenous people's livelihoods. After the polls close, the Bolivians continue to stand by Morales. They don't agree that his casual sweater is shameful to their country, as some observers have commented. Quite the contrary: journalists note that Morales doesn't wear expensive Armani suits like other Latin American leaders — he's one of the people.

President Morales isn't alone. Wool and weaving have been found all over South America. So too has knitting. In fact, according to the knitting historian Richard Rutt, seven indigenous tribes living in the Roraima Mountains, which straddle Venezuela, Guyana, and Brazil in the northeastern corner of South America, may have been the world's first knitters. The Arecuna, the Machushi, the Patamona, and the Taulipang tribes knit headbands, while the Palikur, the Uaca, and the Warrau knit belts. Without hard archaeological facts it's impossible to say whether knitting in South America predates knitting in Egypt or China. But instead of dropping more stitches and neglecting this part of the world, it seems reasonable to say that knitting may have sprouted up simultaneously in Asia, Africa, and the Americas.

We do know for certain that the art of weaving was integral to the Inca civilization in South America. While the Mexihca to the north largely used vegetable fibers like cotton, their neighbors in the Andes also used wool. Andean wool is made from the coats of four lamoids — the llama, the vicuña, the alpaca, and the guanaco. The lamoids, also known as camelids, are related to the camel but indigenous to South America. They generally produce a stronger, warmer, and lighter wool than sheep's wool. The vicuña's fibers are finer and softer than most wool. Wool from the alpaca and its cousins is also free of lanolin — a by-product from sheep's wool that can be used in creams and lotions — making it easier to turn their shorn hair into wool. That's if you can clip or shear the llamas or alpacas without scaring them. When frightened or angered, these Andean creatures spit.

Records show that the people of the Andes domesticated lamoids at least five thousand years ago, though it's possible that they have been using wool for as long as the women of ancient Jarmo in Mesopotamia. When the Spanish invaded, there may have been tens of millions of lamoids in the Andes. Today, there aren't that many in the entire world, even though they are raised for fiber in South America, North America, and Australia. Minnesota, for example, boasts forty-four alpaca farms.

One of these Minnesota lamoid farmers is another grant writer. Wendy's real passion is knitting, something she's been doing since she was seven years old. She learned how to spin in college, and after she graduated she saved up to buy a spinning wheel of her own. It didn't take long before she started thinking, why not have fiber animals of her own? For twenty-one years, she has raised a small flock of llamas about thirty miles north of the Twin Cities because "these critters are my buddies." She's added a few alpacas, whose wool is finer, but they're not as interesting. "My llamas and I can read each other's moods. If I'm upset, my llamas will come up and comfort me. Alpacas just aren't like that." Wendy gets about one sweater and a few pairs of socks from every lamoid she shears. "My closet is full of more yarn than I can handle."

The oldest traces of the Andean use of string are found not in a burial site or on a female miniature sculpture, like the string cloth found in ancient Ukrainian grave sites: they are an ancient form of writing called *quipu*. *Quipus* are systematically tied knots and strings — an alphabet of yarn used to communicate.

Until recently archaeologists dated *quipus* back to about 650 CE. But in 2005, the archaeologist Ruth Shady found a 5,000-year-old *quipu* in the ancient Peruvian city of Caral. The *quipu* consists of a single strand of wool from which hangs hundreds to thousands of other strings, kind of like a mobile. The colors, the levels, the knots, and the arrangements recorded numerical data as well as administrative information and narratives. In other words, the *quipus* were a form of writing, which the Incans used for at least 4,500 years.

Writing wasn't the only use for wool in the Americas. The Incas also used the fiber of their robust lamoids for clothing. While coastal and working people tended to wear cotton, the Inca nobility wore wool. The men wore tunics, and women wore dresses. Both wore cloaks over their undergarments. Inca weaving was so fine that some of their cloth contained six hundred threads to the inch — the finest in existence until the Industrial Revolution and textile machinery.

I find a photograph of an Inca tunic on the Internet. It is

square-shaped, like the one I imagine that Ishtar wore, then removed, on her journey to visit her sister in the Mesopotamian underworld. This one is composed of dozens of small woven squares, like the Hmong *paj ntaub*. Each square is woven with a unique geometric design. They are stitched together like a quilt or an African strip cloth.

There are four colors: red, white, gold, and black — like the colors in the medicine wheel used by indigenous cultures in North America. If you stare at the Inca tunic long enough, it starts to go funny on you, like a trippy Escher drawing. Or at least that's what happens to me. After a while, I can't find my point of origin inside the Incan maze of diamonds and color. I am caught inside the design, twirling around and around, going nowhere.

To prepare for his inauguration as president, Evo Morales participates in an ancient spiritual ceremony to demonstrate his dedication to the indigenous people who constitute two-thirds of Bolivia's population. Along with thousands of supporters, Morales drives to a sacred mountain temple about forty-five miles outside La Paz. There he makes an offering of flowers to the Inca Mother Earth goddess, the Pacha Mama.

Textiles and writing are linked in almost every part of the world. From the Inca *quipu* to the Hmong *paj ntaub* to the clay tablets recording the story of Ishtar's clothes, from the encoded itinerary in the quilts used along the Underground Railroad to the goddess figurines all over Europe who danced in string skirts, textile traditions around the world keep our stories and our culture alive. The knitting we do today extends these stories of survival into our world, too.

When we listen closely enough to our knitting, we can hear what it is trying to say.

I pull out my bamboo needles and continue knitting the first few inches of Evan's sweater front. Leaning in to the gray yarn, I hear encouragement in each stitch. "You can do it," the stitches say. "You and women like you have been knitting and making clothes from wool for thousands of years," they continue. My faith grows, row after row.

Kong's Café

"One time this guy I dated in college asked me if I would stay with him if he were impotent," says Betty, leaning into the booth where three of us are having lunch, a few days before Christmas at Kong's Café on Lake Street, just across the Mississippi River in Minneapolis.

"Hah!" we all laugh in unison.

This is a reunion lunch prompted by Janet's trip to Minneapolis to visit her oldest daughter. Ten years ago, the three of us worked together at the Minneapolis American Indian Center for an after-school Native youth program. I keep reminders of Betty and Janet with me every day. Betty beaded the keychain I use, and Janet gave me a beaded pen. I call it the "miracle pen" because after all these years, the ink still hasn't run dry.

Our laughter over this Christmas lunch balances out the tough things we've been talking about — going through divorce, and figuring out how to balance taking good care of our kids with taking care of ourselves. We talk about our new relationships. Are we falling into old traps or staying true to ourselves?

Betty pushes away her wonton soup and asks, "So how's the keychain — still in good shape?"

"Yeah, it's great. Except, well, I messed it up myself," I say, pulling her handiwork out of my purse. "See here, I accidentally slipped a key under the top row. A few beads are coming loose." We all stare at the keychain. It's shaped like a cylinder, with beads of blues, white, and black forming diagonal streaks of lightning.

"I love how this one shines so much — see that," I say, twisting it around. Even in the dim light of Kong's Café, the beads glisten.

As in Africa, Asia, Europe, and Latin America, the ancient textile traditions of weaving and decorative arts are rich in North America. Beadwork by Ojibwe women like Betty and Janet demonstrates that indigenous women are keeping these traditions alive and well in the twenty-first century.

Long before the Spanish or other Europeans arrived, indigenous people along the northwestern coast of North America made yarn and wove cloth. Their traditions of weaving, some still in use today, resonate with the themes found in fiber history around the world. Like the embroidered Hmong *paj ntaub*, the Pacific tribal weaving told the people's history. Their textiles carried the sacred power of regeneration like the cloak of the Middle Eastern goddess Ishtar. Their weavings were used in sacred dances like those conducted in ancient Europe. Pacific coastal weaving twined the sacred power of the maker with the sacred power of the creator, like that first knitted sock in Egypt. Like the Incas to the south, the Northwest coastal weavers incorporated clean yet mesmerizing geometric designs.

Among the best known of these indigenous Pacific weavers are the Tlingit, who live in present-day western Alaska and Canada. Tlingit weavers are known for being the only people in the world who can weave a perfect circle by hand. Contemporary Tlingit weavers still weave with yarn made from a mix of softened cedar bark, which is rain-resistant, and mountain-goat hair. They weave ceremonial robes worn for dancing in pivotal rituals — births, deaths, marriages — not unlike the Kuba *nchak* dance skirts worn in central Africa.

Like the story of the Hmong, Tlingit history has been preserved for maybe ten thousand years in textiles, through the symbolic designs woven into their robes. This sustained connection between place, craft, and culture offers Tlingit weavers and robe dancers a pathway beyond the boundaries of time. As the weaver and writer Suzi Vaara Williams writes, "These robes represent the heart of the Tlingit People. They represent our ancestors and provide a link, a spiritual connection through time, to our ancestors and the cosmos."[4]

Farther south, the Salish Indians in the U.S. Pacific Northwest had a tradition of weaving blankets from wool made of the fur of a now-extinct dog. They mixed the dog's fine fur with mountain-goat wool, goose down, and sometimes cedar bark. Like the Tlingit farther north, the Salish were quite possibly making and weaving wool at the same time that the women of Jarmo were taking sheep hair and turning it into yarn.

Although the Salish no longer make their own wool,

---

4 Suzi Vaara Williams writes eloquently about her work as a Tlingit weaver in several essays that appear on the Internet, including "The Essence of Chilkat Weaving," http://alaskanativearts.net/suzi/ essence.htm (accessed August 19, 2008).

they continue to produce woolen goods, including sweaters. The modern Salish artist Joe Jack keeps a part of their yarn-making and weaving tradition alive by making modern spindle whorls. The weighted whorl of a handspindle makes it easier to draw out and twist the fibers into yarn. In his contemporary carvings, Joe Jack incorporates ancient Salish designs of humans, animals, and geometric shapes. As the whorl spins, the designs spin too, so fast that the spinner is mesmerized and can fall into a trance. It is said that the spinner then can weave textiles that have special powers.

The Pueblo people in the American Southwest are also heirs to a long tradition of weaving from cotton and yucca fibers, a tradition that likely derived from the well-established art of textiles in Mexico and Central America and existed from at least 700 CE. Diné, or Navajo, immigrants from the Pacific Northwest arrived in the region in the 1300s. They either brought their knowledge of weaving with them or adopted the Pueblo and Mexican style of weaving. When the Spaniards invaded the region in the 1500s, they brought sheep with them from Europe. Both the Pueblo and the Diné began using the sheep fibers to make wool. One historian claims that by 1840, indigenous weavers in the Rio Grande Valley of New Mexico were exporting twenty thousand woven blankets to Mexico every year.

Textile production wasn't restricted to the North American West. Recent archaeological digs have turned up evidence of indigenous weaving all along the eastern seaboard. Like the Ukraine archaeological site, North American indigenous people's burial grounds have yielded woven textile remnants. In Florida, for example, just ten miles from Cape Canaveral, archaeologists found the burial remains of eight thousand bodies in a pond. Many of the bodies were still wrapped in cloth woven from palm fibers. Kathryn Jakes of Ohio State University notes that the construction, design, and weaving of the cloth found all along the U.S. East Coast are so diverse that she believes each region produced its own cloth.[5] These East Coast weavers were also skilled enough to dye their cloth with colors that have held fast for more than a thousand years.

These abundant traditions of weaving in North America reveal another dropped stitch in our shared textile history. I was taught that wool first came into being in Jarmo, Iraq, where Shirlee's grandson is stationed. That's where wool first came into use in the West. But animal fibers have been used for millennia in the Americas, too. Archaeological evidence just isn't available to confirm whose yarn came first. It seems so likely that this tradition of turning animal fiber into a resilient, warm, water-repellent yarn for human clothing belongs to a global family, not a single prizewinner. The Salish and Tlingit of the Pacific Northwest, the tribes on the eastern American seaboard, the Egyptians, the Chinese, and the seven tribes in northeastern South America are sisters in the clan of women who responded to the primal need we all share to clothe our children.

Evidence shows that in the Midwest, the ancestors of the Dakota and the Ojibwe used buffalo and deer hair to make wool. It seems they were more likely to clothe themselves in the hides of animals that lived in the forests and prairies native to our region. Buffalo hide was turned into blankets

---

5 "Scraps of Prehistoric Fabric Provide a View of Ancient Life," Ohio State University Research News, August 22, 2004, http://research news.osu.edu/archive/prefab.htm (accessed September 3, 2008).

and tepees. Deer hide became dresses, bags, and shoes. While the men hunted, the women did the arduous work of tanning the hides and then sewing them into clothing, using bone needles and sinew thread.

Decorating the clothing was also a women's art. Before the French, the fur trade, and European glass beads arrived via the great lakes and forests of northern Minnesota, Native women dyed and sewed porcupine quills into their shoes and clothes. These decorations were not frivolous or secondary to the function of the clothing. Native women's textile arts imbued each piece with meaning and magnified its powers. The decorated clothing gave the wearer both beauty and power.

Minnesota's first peoples created designs similar to the geometric designs of Peru. They made quill stars that danced in their dresses like the stars in a winter night sky. From straight porcupine quills, women also fashioned rounded flowers that grew in the woods and grasslands. When they began using imported glass beads, bright red and pink flowers, lime and kelly green leaves shimmered against a black background. The women's quillwork and beadwork transformed the simplest garment, shoes, or basket into a magnificent constellation of pattern and color.

To this day, young Ojibwe children learn how to bead by copying traditional floral designs. That's how Betty learned, starting out being taught by an Ojibwe bead artist in a program at her elementary school in Minneapolis. When she was Evan's age, Betty had already completed her first piece, a wristband. The incentive, she says, was that she got to take the loom and some beads home after school. Betty continued beading in high school, where one teacher submitted some of her better pieces to a national contest.

Today, at Kong's Café, Betty is not the only artist whose work we admire. Janet pulls out an open-faced square box and sets it on the table. It holds a wallet, beaded in dark blues, with a medicine wheel in the center. The medicine wheel is a circle divided into four, with yellow, black, red, and white pie pieces. Small black-and-white feathers form a border around the edge of the wallet. The beadwork is fine and tight but not shiny. Though it's made from synthetic beads, this piece is obviously made by someone who knows how to bead.

"I made it for my guy, but I don't want to give it to him anymore. Charlie said he'd give me $90 to sell this at his store," says Janet, kind of quiet.

Diego could use a new wallet, and I still haven't found him just the right Christmas present. I open the wallet. It's a nice one, with lots of pockets and card holders inside. But something doesn't feel right about it. Janet senses this and suggests she might be able to finish another one by Christmas.

We leave the café with plans to call each other in a few days. I hop into the Honda, turn the ignition on with Betty's keychain dangling below the steering wheel, drive down Lake Street, and head back to the river.

I love spending time with these two artist friends. Their living traditional art connects me to women who've been spinning, weaving, and decorating textiles for thousands of years on *this* continent. Add in what I've learned about women's textile history around the world, and I can see that women make up the four pie pieces inside Janet's medicine wheel, representing all four major continents — Europe, Asia, Africa, and the Americas. We're white, yellow, black, and red, but we're all inside the circle because we share the skill of making beautiful and powerful the objects necessary for survival. I cross the Lake Street Bridge over the river and hear a ring of laughter circling the earth, an ancient belly laugh of sisterhood. It's time to finish Evan's sweater. Really. I mean it this time.

The Mad Hatter

The leftover glow of lunch at Kong's Café propels me to return to my own craft, knitting. Unlike Janet and Betty, whose beadwork tells the story of their Ojibwe culture in each piece they create, I don't have a direct cultural link to my craft. Still, knitting is my craft of choice, and I find surges of great passion for it. I remember the mixed feelings I had when I began Evan's sweater in October. Joy and fear, working together like my two knitting needles.

I've stayed the course down here in the rabbit hole where I started the project. With the back and two sleeves finished, I'm finding my path through the unknown just as Alice did in Looking-Glass Land. I've discovered curious friends along the way, too. The worshipping weaving women of prehistoric Europe, the yarn makers of Jarmo, Hmong seamstresses, West African weavers, Mexican cotton spirits, Salish spinners, and even a blessed sock knitter in Egypt.

As I start the front and final piece of Evan's sweater, I wonder how knitting made its way from North Africa to

Europe. I wonder who were the women who turned knitting into an art form in the homes of my own ancestors in northern Europe.

It turns out that knitting took one unofficial route and two official routes from Africa to Europe. The first official route was via Egypt, Greece, and Italy. The Egyptians taught the Greeks how to knit after Alexander conquered Egypt in 332 BCE. Two centuries later, Rome conquered Greece, and Greek slaves were put to work weaving and knitting for Romans. The second official route was from North Africa to Spain. When the Moors, or Muslims, of North Africa expanded into Spain beginning in 711 CE, they shared the art and industry of handknitting with their largely Christian Spanish subjects.

Unofficially, of course, knitting and textiles moved across the Mediterranean from one woman's home to the next. Perhaps a Greek slave in Italy showed her master how to knit. A Christian Spaniard may have spied a Moorish Spaniard wearing a beautiful knitted stocking. She copied the method and the design from her neighbor, then taught her own daughter to knit. The master and the daughter taught their neighbors and daughters, who taught their neighbors and daughters, until all of Italy and all of Spain were knitting colorful caps, gloves, and stockings for so many generations that no one now remembers who taught whom. Nor did knitting stop at the Italian and Spanish borders. Remnants of knitted socks, gloves, and waistcoats dating from as early as the 1200s have been found all over Europe.

The Italians, however, seemed to have a special knack for harnessing knitting and weaving. As women began filling their homes with beautiful woolen goods, the Italians birthed a powerful textile industry that made the past Greek textile profiteers look second-rate. Historians say that the profits that Italians made from selling their woven textiles and knitted wares built their nations' powerful banking systems during the Renaissance. Without the textile revenue, there would have been no Medicis, nor the Leonardos, Raphaels, and Michelangelos that these wealthy patrons sponsored. Some of these artists even paid tribute to women knitters in their work. In fact, in Italian painting, and later in German art, knitting is linked to the Christian fertility goddess, Mary.

One of these knitting Madonnas, according to Richard Rutt, appears in a 1345 painting believed to have been done by Ambrogio Lorenzetti of Siena. In it, Mary, Joseph, and Jesus are sitting in a comfortable circle on a carpet. Mary is knitting in the round with four needles. A very young Jesus clutches at her robe, while Joseph gazes at a round tray on the floor, filled with colorful spools of thread set into wooden pins. Presumably, as Mary tugs on each color she needs, the yarn neatly unwinds from its spool. How I wish I had had one of these as I was knitting Evan's sleeve pattern, with three colors going at once.

About fifty years later, the German painter Master Bertram of Minden painted a well-known knitting Madonna called the Buxtehude Madonna, after the Benedictine monastery for which he painted. In this one, Mary and Jesus appear in a room open to the outdoors, with ornate leaded windows and a view of a leafy arbor. Mary is seated next to a simple woven basket holding three balls of yarn, while Jesus sits at a distance on the floor. To the left of them stand two angels carrying a spear, a cross, and a crown of thorns. Jesus looks to be about Evan's age, seven. He's staring away from his mother at the two angels. Mary, meanwhile, is concentrating on knitting a piece in the round. Unlike in the Lorenzetti painting, in which Mary's knitting is only a few inches long, in the Bertram painting we can see what she's knitting — a waistcoat or a wide-waisted shirt with short sleeves. In fact, she's almost finished, just about to knit the neckband — one step ahead of me knitting Evan's sweater.

Italian knitting didn't just adorn the walls of the wealthy Renaissance patrons. Textile profits also funded the first explorations to the New World. Christopher Columbus was the son of a weaver and a part-time weaver himself. It is said he believed that he had struck gold when he landed in Cuba. He didn't mean the valuable metal: he found something better, a storehouse loaded with twelve thousand tons of cotton. Three decades later, Stephen Yafa reports, a local chief gave Hernán Cortés a fine cotton cloth that was woven with strips of real gold.

When I turn my attention to England in the exploration of textiles around the world, I'm reminded of Alice in Wonderland again. In this part of the magical world of textiles I discover one of Alice's contemporaries, the Mad Hatter. The oldest known knitted artifacts found in England are not spiritual socks or divine waistcoats but knitted hats, called "cappers," that date back to the early 1400s. Alice's Mad Hatter is rude and elusive, but on good terms with time. In fact, he can turn time backward and forward at will. If he were here, perhaps he could set his watch back and help clear up the mystery of just how England's textile industry grew from a single cap to the largest international enterprise in the world.

The British seem to have gotten a jump start in the early 1300s, when Flemish weavers crossed the Channel to escape a Spanish invasion. In less than fifty years, England started selling wool and woven goods back to Germany, France, and even Spain. To honor the growing importance of wool in England, King Edward II introduced the Woolsack into Parliament in the mid-1300s. The Woolsack is a pillow woven and stuffed with wool that serves as a seat for the lord chancellor (a bit like the speaker of the U.S. House of Representatives). He still sits on the Woolsack in the British parliament today, although presumably after seven hundred years there is new stuffing in the pillow.

In the 1400s, King Edward III introduced more stringent laws to protect the English wool trade from foreign competition. Meanwhile, peasants on large estates were put to work making woolen cloth in their cottages when they weren't working in the fields. Whole families knit for hours each day in their dark, smoky cottages and supplemented their meager income as farmers by selling socks, gloves, caps, vests, and petticoats to their lords and ladies. These were the original cottage "sweat-ers," who never lived to see or wear what we call a sweater today.

The English knitting business took another step forward under Queen Elizabeth, who reigned from 1558 to 1603. Under her leadership, England set up knitting schools, where young girls were trained and then paid to knit even more than their parents could at home. With their adolescent energy, nimble fingers, and sharper eyesight, they could knit a single sock in just eight hours.

Queen Elizabeth was famous for her love of luxury goods, including silk Spanish socks. Not all her subjects appreciated the queen's love of finery. The English poet George Gascoigne wrote a poem in 1575 that describes the decadence and sacrilege of Queen Elizabeth's court, "our knit silk stocks . . .

provoking filthy pride, and snares unseen which lead a man to Hell."[6]

However, detractors didn't stop Queen Elizabeth from amassing knitted silk stockings; nor did they slow the boom in the English wool business. By 1660, woolen goods accounted for two-thirds of all of England's exports. Weaving and wool had become big business, one that helped fuel England's own colonial pursuits and eventually outpaced those of the Italians they had carefully studied.

How did the English take over? An invention by the husband of a knitter is said to have fueled the growth of Britain's textile industry. Purportedly driven mad by the sounds of his wife's knitting needles clacking away, William Lee invented the knitting machine to make for quieter evenings at home. Knitting production, which had been sparse like a light dusting of snow across the cottages dotting Yorkshire Dales, sped up over the next several centuries until it roared like a Minnesota blizzard in December.

The British empire realized that it had to keep a constant watch on its wool industry, especially in its colonies — the Crown's economic lifeblood. Though India had been producing its own cloth for thousands of years before the English arrived, the English restricted Indian weaving production and required instead that Indians import cloth made in England. Closer to home, Ireland had started a robust weaving industry. Because wages there were lower, the Irish began to undercut English prices. Britain dealt with Irish competition by enacting several new policies designed to reduce Irish woolen

---

6 Quoted in Richard Rutt, *A History of Hand Knitting* (Loveland, CO: Interweave Press, 1989), 69.

production in the 1690s. For instance, the 1699 Wool Act declared that Ireland could export woolen goods to just one country — Britain. The British did, however, let the Irish weave linen, something for which Ireland is still famous today.

Did Britain face the same pressures to maintain their textile edge in a third colony — that new land we call America? The answer will have to wait until I get a little further along on the front of Evan's sweater. If only I could invite Alice's grumpy friend the Mad Hatter for tea, I'd ask him to turn back time so I could finish the sweater by Christmas morning.

Right-Hand Men

I am whipping through the front of Evan's sweater now. I have to. There are just five days until Christmas. To give me a fighting chance, I enlist the boys as my helpers. I tell them that they are going to have to be my right-hand men.

This strategy works well at this time of year. They both look forward to getting presents. Andrew helps load up the dishes after dinner. Evan cleans up his room. They go outside for a snowball fight. I get time to knit — before dinner, after dinner, and on the weekend. At ninety-two stitches across, it's slow going for me, even with a simple stockinette pattern and just one color of yarn. By sticking firm to my goal, I take my place in a long line of American knitters who have knit with a purpose.

The first colonists in America had a different purpose when they knit: independence. Like India and Ireland, the American colonies posed a threat to England's wool industry. Early on, the Crown had forbidden colonists to export sheep to America. However, the few sheep that had been smuggled out of the country had grown to a flock of about one hundred thousand by 1665. The Americans began to knit socks and undergarments and to sell them locally at prices lower than those of imported English clothes. The colonists in America didn't build their wool industry just for profit: they complained that the imported woven socks were uncomfortable and didn't fit well. The Crown fought back by imposing more laws in the 1700s, even outlawing the transport of wool or woolen goods within the Americas. Anyone found guilty of trading in wool was subject to punishment: King George III ordered their right hands to be cut off.

Fortunately, King George didn't end up cutting off too many American hands or fingers. In the American colonies, unlike in India, the British didn't have a tight administrative structure in place. Moreover, unlike the Irish, the American colonists had a vast ocean protecting them from British interference. So the colonists kept on producing wool. Massachusetts was so defiant that it passed a law *requiring* young people to spin and weave. Some historians believe King George's 1699 Wool Act was one of the most important catalysts for the American Revolution.

After the United States gained independence, George Washington and Thomas Jefferson, who both raised sheep, are said to have worn woolen suits at their presidential inaugurations as a symbol of freedom. Two centuries later, Mohandas Gandhi spun and wore his own handwoven cotton cloth, leading a nonviolent Indian economic rebellion against the English. More recently, of course, the newly elected Bolivian president Evo Morales began wearing his red, white, and blue–striped sweater to official events. When he appeared on Jon Stewart's *Daily Show*, Morales wore a woolen jacket trimmed with red woven piping, leading his twenty-first-century economic rebellion in traditional indigenous cloth, too.

Fifty years after the United States gained independence from England, the American textile industry began to take off. In 1812, James Cabot Lowell traveled to Manchester, England, the center of Britain's wool industry, where the original homemade knitting machine had expanded into giant factory-sized looms and the average lifespan of a mill worker was just seventeen years. (In fact, so grim was life in the mills that it inspired the son of one mill owner, Friedrich Engels, to write *The Condition of the Working Class in England* and started him along the path that would lead to his collaboration with Karl Marx.) English laws prevented Lowell from exporting drawings of the mechanized mills, so he memorized the entire workings of the water-powered loom. When he returned, he helped found one of America's first industrial mill towns: Lowell, Massachusetts, on the Merrimack River.

Young, educated rural women streamed into Lowell to work in the new mills. They worked long hours, six and a half days a week, at very low wages. But unlike factory workers in England, the New England girls gained a level of independence. As one Lowell worker wrote:

> One who sits on my right hand at table is in the factory because she hates her mother-in-law.... The next one has a wealthy father but like many of our country farmers, he is very penurious... the next is here because her parents are wicked infidels... the next is here because she has been ill-treated in so many families she has a horror of domestic service ... the next has left a good home because her lover, who has gone on a whaling voyage, wishes to be

married when he returns, and she would like more money than her father will give her.[7]

Before long, the output of the looms and mills of the eastern seaboard rivaled that of England's industrial cities. England saw an opportunity to regain its dominance during the American Civil War, aligning with the American South, where enslaved labor had planted, picked, and produced cotton. In the end, Britain didn't join the South, and the United States won the textile race. Planned towns like Lawrence, Massachusetts, upstream from Lowell on the Merrimack River, sprang up all over New England. By the 1880s, the American mills had to look for more laborers to meet the growing demand for U.S. textiles. The mills advertised for workers, and soon immigrants from Italy, Ireland, Russia, and eastern Europe, eager to work, poured into the mill towns. Machines sped up. Production reached a fever pitch.

Working conditions worsened inside the New England mills. There was little light, little ventilation, and a constant, deafening roar of machinery. Workers were not allowed to go to the bathroom at will and had little time to eat. The speeding machines forced them to work faster than was safe. Many fingers and hands — and even scalps — were lost. The workers began organizing to campaign for better conditions. The famous Bread and Roses strike erupted in Lawrence in 1912, after the machines had been sped up 50 percent and the wages cut to the point that workers could buy five fewer loaves of bread each week to feed their families. Young female strikers carried banners that read, "We want bread and roses, too."

---

7 Harriet Farley, "Letters from Susan: Fourth Letter," *Lowell Offering* 4 (September 1844): 257–59. See also the website of Old Sturbridge Village, Inc., www.osv.org.

For ten weeks, twenty thousand men and women encircled the mills, enduring hunger and brutality from police, who used hoses to deluge the strikers with water in the frigid January weather. The government sided with the textile companies until one congressional hearing attended by President William Taft's wife. She listened as an immigrant teenager named Camella Teoli explained why she started working in the mill, even though she was underage:

> Well, I used to go to school, and then a man came up to my house and asked my father why I didn't go to work, so my father says I don't know whether she is 13 or 14 years old. So the man say you give me $4 and I will make papers come from the old country saying you are 14. So father gave him the $4, and in one month came the papers that I was 14. I went to work and about two weeks [later] got hurt in my head. The machine pulled my scalp off.[8]

Camella's testimony made headlines across the nation. After ten weeks of linking arms, the workers, who between them spoke twenty-seven different languages, won concessions from the woolen companies. They received a 25 percent raise for the lowest-paid workers, overtime pay, and an assurance that strikers would get their jobs back. The changes affected not only the lives of young women like Camella but also the lives of the other 250,000 textile workers in New England. Conditions were still grim, however. One Lowell

---

8 History Matters: The U.S. Survey Course on the Web, American Social History Project/Center for Media and Learning, City University of New York and Center for History and New Media at George Mason University, http://historymatters.gmu.edu/d/61 (accessed August 15, 2008).

mill worker in the 1920s said of the weaving room, "It was the noisiest room you could ever be in. There's machines going and shuttles going back and forth, and sometimes they'd fly off and they were pointed things and if they ever hit you, boy, you'd know it. The whole place vibrates. When I came out of there at night I was shaking."[9]

Conditions weren't much better in the newer cotton mills in the American South, which had lagged behind their northern counterparts until the strikes starting brewing in the north. In the southern mills, wages could still be held low without fear of strikes. White men were paid the highest wages, black men the least for doing the hardest work — carrying bales of cotton between the rail cars and the factories. African American women were excluded from working in the southern mills altogether. However, southern workers began to assert themselves, too. A string of southern textile strikes in the 1930s culminated in the 1934 general strike in which more than four hundred thousand workers walked off the job along the southeastern seaboard. Though this was the largest labor conflict in American history, the companies held firm with the help of privately hired militias. Franklin D. Roosevelt sent in a little help for the workers — too late, because he needed the southern Democrat vote to pass the New Deal. Eventually the southern workers conceded. Many of them were permanently blacklisted and unable to return to their jobs.

A few years ago I discovered that my family has connections to both sides of the 1912 strike in Lawrence. After

---

9 "Lowell National Historical Park: Decline and Recovery," Lowell National Historical Park, www.nps.gov/archive/lowe/loweweb/Lowell _History/decline.htm (accessed August 15, 2008).

emigrating from Ireland to East Boston, a great-great-grandfather of mine later moved his family and small construction business north to Lawrence in the early 1900s. In Lawrence, the Murphys could take advantage of the mill-driven economic boom. However, they didn't help to build the mills. Textile companies like the American Wool Company refused to house Irish Catholic immigrants in the company dormitories. So, with the help of his two sons, Mr. Murphy and his construction company built tenements for the immigrant mill workers.

Then Mr. Murphy lost his two right-hand men. My great-great-uncle left the trades to become a police officer, a police detective, and finally a company inspector for the mills — contributing his knowledge of building codes to the textile industry. His brother, my great-grandfather, didn't want to climb the economic ladder like his brother. He didn't like the way the police and the mill owners collaborated to keep profits high at the expense of the immigrant workers. So he left Lawrence before the mills went up in flames and before the Bread and Roses strike, and headed west to quarry granite in Minnesota.

I am not an indigenous weaver or a revolutionary knitter stitching for freedom. I am not a mill worker in Lowell or Lawrence. Nor am I an inspector turning a blind eye to the fire hazards and working conditions in the textile mills. I am a twenty-first-century American woman knitting a sweater by choice. This choice incorporates the knowledge that making garments can be an act of defiance, or a desperate act of survival, for far too many Americans. I am desperate, too, but in a different way. I am desperate to finish Evan's sweater. I am still counting on my two right-hand men, Andrew and Evan, to buy me enough time to finish by Christmas.

Narnia

A couple of days later, I wake up feeling horrible. I don't want to get out of bed, but the boys and I have a special Christmas date planned with my sister, Cate, that I don't have the heart to break. We'll have a banana-split party at her house and then go to a movie at the Highland Theater.

I pull on my bathrobe and my blue birthday slippers with the feeling of a pernicious weight pushing me down. I feel dizzy and very dry of mouth. At first I think, "Coffee. I need coffee, and then I'll be all right." But no amount of double dark espresso French roast wakes me up this morning. By the time we leave to go to Cate's apartment, the whole adventure seems like an ordeal, not a treat. What is wrong with me?

I try to smile as the boys eat their banana splits (Andrew without the banana, Evan without the nuts). After Cate cleans up, we head down the Montreal hill to the theater to see this season's blockbuster, *The Chronicles of Narnia: The Lion, the Witch and the Wardrobe*. I'm looking forward to it because it's a movie we can all enjoy together. After we pick out our seats, I go to the restroom and take a seat on the cold toilet. Blood — that brown thick mucous that comes at the beginning of the cycle — appears everywhere, on my under-pants and on the toilet lid and in the watery pot below. My period is five days early. It is going to be a rough cycle, arriv-ing when I least want to be weak — just two days before Christmas.

My knitting has hit an unexpected rough patch, too. At 10¾ inches into Evan's front, I'm almost done. I switch from gray to red to knit the bold stripe that will encircle him when the sweater is complete. I get cavalier and knit without double-checking the pattern. Then I cut off the red with the scissors, leaving just a small amount to weave in the end. I switch back to charcoal gray and get started on the top of the front piece. A few rows later, I frown. Something's not right. What? I lay the finished back piece next to this front piece. "Shit," I mutter. The red stripe in this front piece is narrower than the one in the back. The two pieces won't match when I sew them together.

I take off my glasses and lean in close to the finished back sweater piece. I count the number of rows in the red stripe. Four rows. Then I count the red stripe in the front. There I've knit only three. That means I will have to take out the new gray rows and add a fourth row of red. I pull out the stitches in gray and tie the red end to the red ball of yarn. Okay, this isn't so bad, I think, knitting the fourth red row. But this time as I switch back to gray, I see that the knot where I had tied the two red ends together shows on the right side of the sweater. This means tearing out the charcoal and part of the fourth red row again. Forget it, I think. I'm just not going to do this now. I can't.

Until I had children, I never even really noticed my period. It came when it wanted to, lasted just a few days, and never, ever slowed me down. Once Andrew and then Evan were born, I began to pay more attention to my period — learning to tell when I was ovulating by the pinch that came mid-month. I noticed that I had more energy before I ovulated. I enjoyed the release that comes with the flow time of the cycle.

When I turned forty, my cycle got so heavy that I began to feel I was having a miscarriage, month after month after month. I go through slacks and underpants and even chair seats in a hurry, and have to think about how I'm going to get from point A to point B on some days. I finally went to see my doctor. It turns out I am entering the premenopausal stage of life. Not every woman experiences it with heavy blood flow, but some do.

On this chilly late-December Sunday afternoon, my period has beat me to the punch. The movie is already running when I find the boys in the theater. I lean over to Cate to explain why I've been gone so long. "Oh no!" she says in sympathy. As the movie unfolds, I think more about the rhythm of the seasons and women's menstrual cycle. Circles all around — all threaded together by our stories of what it means to be alive, to be human. C. S. Lewis's *Narnia* story is just one example.

The movie adaptation tells of four British children who are removed from the bombing in London during World War II to live in the countryside. In their temporary home, they discover the magical world of Narnia and help to rescue it from the wicked White Witch. When I read the book as a child, the White Witch didn't scare me, but the White Witch in the movie is terrifying. Her skin and dress are deathly white. Her eyes are as piercing and as cold as the eternal snow that her magic casts over Narnia. I'm glad I know the ending ahead of time: the four children bring Narnia back to life with the help of the tawny lion named Aslan.

For C. S. Lewis, Aslan represents Christ. But he could also represent Leo, the astrological symbol that rules the end of summer. He is the patriarchal god arriving to put the goddess under his dominion, as Zeus dominated the Greek female deities. I let the misogyny in this story go for today. Isn't there a lesson to take from Narnia's wintry death sentence? Haven't we heard something like this before? When Ishtar goes to the underworld, life on earth dies. Ishtar's sister returns her clothing and lets her return to earth. Tlazolteotl dives deep into the dark and the soil before she returns with greater strength than before. Both ancient Mesopotamia and ancient Mexico understood this basic human need to take the time to gestate in the dark to bring fertility to the earth. Their life stories show us how to find and appreciate a balance between the dark and the light.

We need light and we need dark. We need the sun and we need the moon. We need the winter solstice, when the world is held in darkness, regaining energy inside the earth's fiery core. Yet we also need the summer solstice, when the world radiates its fullness. The women of old Europe named all of these different aspects of life — birth and death; regeneration and renewal. Hmong women celebrate this cycle every November at the New Year — wearing an heir to the ancient string skirt and preparing their community for a new beginning.

Women's monthly cycles are not so different. Ovulation is like the summer solstice, when we have our peak energy and fertility. But if we were fertile all the time, we might have overpopulated the earth long ago. So the potential energy for life wanes, ebbing as our menstrual blood flows. Yet as we give birth to this death, we make way for new life. We regenerate over the next two weeks, preparing once again for ovulation and birth.

The Hollywood rehashing of the ancient cycle of light and dark, of strength and weakness, helps me make it through to Christmas. I enjoy the quietness inside my body. I survive not by "doing" anything in particular, but by respecting the energy of my monthly cycle and of the universal circle of life. The only drawback is that I don't have the strength to finish knitting the front of Evan's sweater. I'm not going to finish in time for Christmas.

Magicians

The boys, Diego, and I have just returned from Christmas Eve dinner at my parents' house. The red blinking light in the kitchen is not a Christmas decoration. It's the phone alerting me to a new message. Janet called while we were gone. The new beaded wallet is ready. I'm going to have a present for Diego, but not the one I wanted to give to Evan. After all my efforts, I haven't finished Evan's sweater in time for presents by the Christmas tree tomorrow morning.

Even though I am a lapsed Catholic, I love Christmas. The songs, the stockings, the cookies, the tree, the shopping, the secrets, the wreath are all pieces of the pattern that is Christmas, just as any communal ritual forms a pattern of color, actions, and meaning. Of course, I wasn't born with an innate sense of Christmas or how to celebrate it; I was trained into it. Take Christmas stockings. My Grandmother Murphy handknit a new Christmas stocking at the birth of each of her sixteen grandchildren. My stocking has a Santa Claus head that's so big it stretches from the heel to the cuff, and Santa wears a brass bell at the end of his cap. My sister's stocking has a Santa Claus popping out of a chimney. He has a soft white mohair beard that I always preferred to my own Santa's beard. My brother's stocking is a snowman, with a black cap and two red button eyes.

My mother also has a gift for passing along rituals. I watched her knit and make Christmas cookies. When I was a child, she seemed all-powerful wielding her metal knitting needles or rolling out a batch of refrigerated dough. She was powerful because she transformed things from one form into another — flour and sugar into red-nosed-reindeer cookies, a ball of yarn into a knitted sweater.

I can still see my mother sitting on the loveseat in our old living room, her long metal needles click-clacking away around dinnertime. With a hamburger, noodle, and tomato hot dish warming in the oven, my mother would carry on a conversation while knitting. She'd look her audience straight in the eye, yet her hands never stopped moving.

We arrive in the world as observers, but at some point we want to jump in and affect the world. I observed it in Andrew and Evan. Between about ages three and five, both boys wanted to be superheroes. I remember taking Andrew to a grocery store when he was four, dressed in a Batman outfit. In the frozen-food section we ran into another little Batman. The two boys just stared at each other and then turned away, back into their parallel imaginary worlds.

Girls don't get into the superhero thing as much as boys do. We don't want to change ourselves so much as we want to transform objects in the world around us. At least, that's how it was for me. It started in fourth grade. That year my best friend, Alice, and I couldn't stop reading books about witches — like *The Witch of Blackbird Pond* by Elizabeth George Speare. Then we started devouring books with actual spells in them. The next step was to cast the spells. We'd sit on the third floor of her silver-gray Victorian house and whisper spells to turn a bronze doorknob from across the room, or to set fire to grass without matches. Our spells never worked.

But my mother could weave spells at Christmas. She bent garlands into a circle and adorned the wreath with four candles that stayed put on our dining room table for a full month before Christmas. She took an ordinary pine tree and turned it into a spectacle of color and light.

The most magical Christmas of all was the year my mother knit something for each of five people — her three children, husband, and father-in-law — without any one of us ever knowing about our own gift. In the months leading up to that Christmas, whenever one of us came upon my mother, she was knitting something for someone else.

I did not inherit the ease with which my mother created Christmas traditions or knitted goods. I struggled through home economics. My mother used to make at least six different kinds of Christmas treats every year. I'm lucky to get one batch of Christmas cookies done to set out for Santa by Christmas Eve. As children, we awoke to my mother's sparkling Christmas tree. The tree in the skinny blue house by the river takes a week to decorate. I will not finish even one knitting project in time for Christmas.

I have a theory that my lack of domestic skills isn't the only reason that I struggle to make Christmas rituals come alive in the home where I'm raising my kids. Unlike my mother, I involve my boys in every step. That means that when we're decorating cookies, they are there helping me sift the flour, break the eggs, and cream the butter and sugar. The kitchen becomes a disaster scene. When we're trying to decorate the tree, Evan and Andrew start arguing over who gets to hang the white bell with all the shiny mirrors and who gets the golden reindeer. Tension, not tinsel, spreads around the tree.

My mother did much of her work alone. Like a magician, she stood on the stage of transformation, organizing all of the stage props until they were in perfect position. We were the audience. When the curtains rose, we gasped in awe.

On Christmas morning this year, the boys wake up a little after eight o'clock — very reasonable, I think as I nudge Diego. We emerge from our warm bed, and I slip on my bathrobe and blue fuzzy slippers to head downstairs. While I make a pot of coffee, Evan and Andrew admire the wrapped presents with restraint, but begin pulling out the goodies stuffed inside their stockings. I listen. They like the mini-flashlights, but I hear sighs when they pull out the orange I add year after year. When the coffee is ready, we all four take a place by the fireplace — left cold on purpose because Evan still believes in Santa. We open our gifts, with laughter as plentiful as the piles of wrapping paper growing around our chairs. I'm the only one with regrets. Evan's sweater isn't among the wrapped gifts. I am no magician.

Later in the day, the magician's curtains do rise. Janet stops by on Christmas afternoon. The boys are downstairs in the basement with Diego, putting the finishing touches on Santa's big gift this year — an air-hockey table. I've just put a turkey in the oven and set the table for supper with our extended family.

Janet steps inside and hands me a box. I open it. Her wallet shines in the early afternoon sunlight. She's copied her mom's design again — the medicine wheel at the center and the feathers around the edge — but switched some of the colors. As promised, the background is a light turquoise green, not dark blue. I lift the wallet out of the box and press it between my hands. It is soft and warm.

"Thank you, Janet. Thank you," I say, stunned by the wallet's beauty and by the magic she has done with her beads.

Janet also hands me a beaded pink bracelet. "And this is for you, so you can have a little more hot pink in your life."

Our laughter echoes in the 8-degree afternoon when Janet steps back outside. I carry the warmth of our conversation back into the house and take out Evan's sweater. Maybe I can finish the front today. My family won't arrive for a few more hours. I forge ahead, trying to ignore the anger I feel at myself for not finishing in time for Christmas morning. I follow the directions for shaping the neck along the top of the front. There's no one to distract me this afternoon, no boys to involve or audience to appease.

When Diego emerges from the basement after a round of air hockey with the boys, I set down the sweater and hand him his gift. It's late, but not too late. Diego lifts up the box lid and stares in silence at the beaded circle. He, too, is stunned. "Thank you, baby, thank you," he repeats over and over as he opens and closes the beaded wallet. Janet's strength and artistry beam from the work.

I reflect on differences among the textile magicians I know — my mother, Janet, and Elizabeth, who knit Evan's first sweater. My mom was raised in an era when women were expected to be homemakers, full-time and more. Domestic sciences were survival sciences. My mom stopped working when she got married, taking it up again only after my younger brother started school.

By the time Janet and I were approaching our teens, the Equal Rights Amendment was being debated in Congress. The ERA didn't pass, but its effects were dramatic. We became the first generation of American wonder women, raising kids and working outside the home. We had few role models to turn to.

Believing in equal rights, of course, doesn't mean all women have equal gifts. My friends have a natural knack for making beautiful things; I don't. They have chosen to blend work and crafting with a heavier emphasis on their crafts. Elizabeth, in fact, stopped working and chose to take care of her kids full-time. That choice also gave her more time to knit. Like me, Janet has always balanced it all — work, kids, and craft. I've put a heavier emphasis on work because working comes more easily to me than crafting or taking care of the home. The next generation of mothers may regard moms like Janet and me as models for designing their own delicate balance between work and home. Perhaps this balance can arise from honestly acknowledging our challenges and failures. Rather than hide them shamefully, we can recycle them from the deep dark to bring forward new models for motherhood.

The realization that we're still figuring out this balance soothes my anger at myself for not finishing in time. It doesn't make the knitting any easier, though. To form the front neck, I've got to decrease stitches in three places at once — along the right- and left-hand edges and in the center. I can't understand the directions in the pattern no matter how many times

I reread them. Rather than acknowledge the challenge here and wait, gestating in the dark like Ishtar or Tlazolteotl, I fake it until I've got the right number of final stitches at the top of the piece. The shape doesn't quite match the drawing in the boy's sweater pattern. Too bad, I tell myself, getting up to check on the turkey. I may lack my mother's timing and Janet's delivery, but the front of Evan's sweater is done.

The Neck

JANUARY

Loose Ends

I'm proud to report that I've sewn the front and back pieces of Evan's sweater together, leaving the arms unattached until the neck is complete. In the whirlwind of Christmas, however, I've left loose ends running wild, like the clipped strands of yarn sprouting from all four pieces. I'm happy when January arrives and I can get everything back in order, like weaving in the loose ends of the sweater.

A week after Christmas, I take down the tree and put the living-room furniture back in its proper place. I make my way through the four different piles of laundry — still dirty; washed but not dried; dried but not folded; and folded but not put away. And I discover that the boys need jeans. Since the last purchase, Evan's jeans are now too tight around his waist. Andrew's jeans have huge gaps in the knees that make for extra-cool walks home from school.

We usually shop for clothes at second-hand stores, like my old favorite, Ragstock. But it's a challenge to find thrift-store jeans for young boys that fit and are in good condition.

We head out for Valu-Thrift in the old Sun Ray Shopping Mall in St. Paul. I always liked the name. I imagined a Latin American sun god watched over the place. This is his season. The waxing of his solar energy in the north country doesn't make for warmer days yet, but it's already staying light until after five PM.

We don't find jeans at Valu-Thrift today, so we hop back into the shivering car and head for Old Navy, lured there by the post-Christmas ads. Unlike the Sun Ray Shopping Center, the Quarry is just a few years old. It's named after an old granite quarry that once stood here, though not the one that my great-grandfather Murphy worked after he left Massachusetts. I feel sad for the granite boulder that sits in the middle of a half-dozen big-box stores. It looks like one of the boulders that Cuchulainn abandoned in the sea between Ireland and Scotland. This huge rock, framed by a small red metal arch, is barely noticeable among its new neighbors. I stare out at the orange, blue, and red buildings competing for our attention. They are definitely not aurora borealis, or the northern lights, guiding us toward wisdom in the winter sky.

At Old Navy, the choices for boys' jeans overwhelm us. It takes half an hour to narrow it down to the number of pairs I think they need to last until summer. Once the boys are done, I start looking for a pair of pants for myself. As I browse through the women's slacks, I hear them playing some imaginary fighting game over in the boys' section. No luck with pants for me, though I spot a pair of red wool-polyester blend socks sprinkled with colorful dots. I put them on top of the pile of jeans in the cart and swing around to collect the boys. As the three of us head for the checkout line, I notice a display of boys' sweaters. They're adorable, with lots of colorful stripes and patterns. The cost? Nineteen dollars, less than one-third of the price of the yarn and needles I bought at Borealis Yarns to knit Evan's flame sweater.

The textile industry in the United States continued to change long after the days of Lawrence and Lowell. The Greeks found it profitable to break up female-headed, home-based weaving enterprises, and the English found it profitable to export cloth woven in the Manchester mills to their colonies around the world. More recently, American clothing companies have begun to increase their profits by using labor and cloth from abroad. This strategy results in lower prices for the American consumer. Believe me, I'm grateful. Boys' jeans are on sale for sixteen dollars at Old Navy this week. An intricate, albeit machine-woven, sweater costs just nineteen dollars. If I can't figure out how to finish Evan's sweater, I might come back and buy one.

But there is a price that doesn't show up on the tag when I buy new clothes in the American mall — the price paid every day by the people who made these sweaters and jeans. Garments made in sweatshops around the world line the clothing racks of the United States. The modern-day sweaters from Mexico and Central America are the daughters of Tlazolteotl, the spirit mother of cotton. They endure working conditions similar to those that Camella Teoli faced at the time of the Bread and Roses strike in Lawrence.

Take Yesenia Bonilla of Honduras, who started her job before she was legally old enough to work, just like Camella:

> I started working at the factory when I was sixteen. I live with six brothers and sisters, as well as my father and mother; and my sister's daughter. When you're the oldest in a large family there's not much choice but to work to support the family. So I left school to help out. It wasn't easy to get the job. The women in

charge of hiring said, "No, little one, you are too young," and escorted me right out of the industrial park. It was three months before I managed to get them to hire me. I got to know one of the guards at the park, and he snuck me in one day. My mother was working there. And by that time there was a new director of personnel. He took one look at me and said, "You're very young, but I'll see what I can do." He gave me some tests and when he saw that I could do the work, he gave me my needle. That's how I got into the maquila at sixteen.[1]

Like Camella, she suffered a lot of hardship once on the job:

We endured a lot of abuse. We started work at 7 in the morning and wouldn't finish until late at night. There was no scheduled time when our shift ended. That made it very difficult for people who lived far away. Another problem was that the company didn't provide purified water. The water was really dirty. But the worst problem was how they treated us. Supervisors would hit us with fabric pieces. They'd throw them in our faces and swear at us.

Since the mid-1990s, however, the workers in Mexico and Central America have started organizing for better working conditions. Yesenia and her coworkers won concessions. These, however, were temporary, just as the mill owners once retracted their promises in Lawrence.

---

1 Quoted in Liza Featherstone and United Students against Sweatshops, *Students against Sweatshops* (London: Verso, 2002), 75–76, 76, 77, 78.

In 1994, we decided to organize a union.... We did make some gains. We got purified water; the company started to pay for transportation and they also fixed the road to the factory. They put in lights so it wasn't so dark for those who had to walk home late at night. But it didn't take long before they forgot all that and started treating us badly again. In 1996, we started to organize again.... That's when we called a strike.

Camella and Yesenia have counterparts outside the Americas. Many sweatshops, or *maquilas*, in Mexico are already closing up shop because wages have risen too high for the companies to sustain their profits. New clothing factories are opening up in China. When that gets too expensive, they'll move to Mongolia or Mali, where women's labor is still plentiful and cheap, at least for now. The pursuit of profit seems like human nature to an entrepreneur, just as the pursuit of sturdy clothes at good prices comes naturally to someone who buys, rather than makes, most of her clothes. The textile industry engaged slave weavers in Greece and Rome; peasants in smoky Yorkshire cottages; child mill workers in Manchester, England; educated farm girls in Lowell; Italian and Irish immigrants in Lawrence; and mothers and daughters in Latin America.

I can't weave in the loose ends of these economic cycles that cause suffering across time and place. I can't stop them. Worse than that, I help keep them going. I am a working American mother who has to clothe her kids. I will continue to buy clothes at Ragstock and other secondhand stores when I can find clothes that fit the boys. But I will also continue to buy clothes at Old Navy when I can't. I hate knowing that my

purchases depend on pain endured by Yesenia and her counterparts in sweatshops around Latin America and Asia. I feel
helpless because our global economy doesn't offer us better
options, options that would provide clothing and economic
justice to all families in the world.

Knitting a pair of socks or knitting a sweater hardly seems
like much of a solution to this injustice. But knitting for a
loved one takes us a little way beyond the margins of suffering in the textile industry. Right now all I can do is weave the
gray and red and golden ends into the pieces of Evan's
sweater. So that's exactly what I do. I thread a fat needle again
and again with each dangling end and braid each one into the
fabric of Evan's sweater.

As I work, I remember Camella. I think about Yesenia
and her next shift at the factory, praying that the lights are on
in the lane when she leaves to catch her bus home in the dark
of a Central American evening. Awareness, prayers, and a few
stitches aren't going to start a revolution in the global textile
market, but they're a step in a more compassionate direction.

The Rescue

It's a quiet evening. The boys have gone to their dad's house to celebrate New Year's, and the temperature has been dropping all day. Diego and I sit by a roaring fire, eating a fancy meal for the two of us: grilled chicken sausage, scrambled eggs, and fried potatoes — a far cry from our usual quick quesadillas or twin bowls of cold cereal and milk when the boys are gone. Snow is on its way. Like Bee, my colleague at the Hmong community agency, used to say, "You can just feel it in your bones, can't you?" Yes, I can. The marrow of my bones gets a ticklish feeling, almost like goose bumps, when it's about to snow.

After dinner Diego takes out a book, and I take out my knitting. My goal is to knit the neck before the boys return on Monday after school. I pull out the circular knitting needle I've been saving for this last task. Then I take the front and back pieces. Although they are sewn at the tops of the shoulders, both pieces have fringes of loose stitches around the neck opening, waiting to be knit up on the circular needle. I review the directions from the little boy's sweater pattern, picking up the stitches from each piece as they instruct me. I don't have a clue what to do. But this doesn't stop me from getting started. There's just too much good energy here by the fire on this almost snowy winter night to wait any longer.

As we sit in silence, my sense of self starts dissolving like it did at the Samhain New Year's bonfire so many years ago, when the fire was calling me home. Tonight, the fire is calling both Diego and me. In this shared quiet, we are no longer physical bodies tied to the earth. The flames leap out and gather us in their airy hands. They draw us in through the glass grate, and we merge into the fire. Neither one of us needs to say a word. We know that the elements will churn our bodies and our spirits like the alchemists of old until we transform into the most elemental form of all — pure energy.

In this pure energy, I start knitting, forming a circle with the front and back pieces. First, I resurrect old stitches from the sweater front, sliding each one carefully onto the needle. Done, with care. Next, the pattern says, "Pick up 11 sts along left neck edge." I take my glasses off and squint at this side of the back. This piece is much too small to fit eleven stitches. But this is not a night to be obstructed by physical limitations. Somehow I pick up eleven stitches. The pattern tells me to add the back stitches. Oh, those patient stitches, tied off on a piece of red yarn for two months! I untie the yarn and slip each back stitch onto the circular needle. Finally, I add eleven more stitches from the other side of the front.

When the stitches around the circular needle are all picked up, I stop, amazed. The neckband is like the medicine wheel on Janet's beaded wallet. Multiple pieces merge into one through the power of the circle. I knit a few rows around the circle in the color that Evan asked for, the goldenrod yellow. This circle will have the power to connect Evan to the flames of Samhain. It will connect him to the elemental energy of life. I set the circle down and breathe. Baking in the waning glow of the fire, I am pure joy.

A thick coat of snow covers the ground when I wake the next morning and look out the window of our pink bedroom. It's beautiful. I rush downstairs to heat up water for coffee and check on the sweater. I expect to find the beauty I'd left the night before. Instead, a lumpy narrow oval greets me, bearing no resemblance to the sweater pattern or to Janet's perfect medicine wheel.

What was I thinking last night?

I toss the deformed neck into my little knitting basket and try to ignore it for a few days. I can't. I obsess about it constantly, wondering how in the world Evan is going to feel when he finds out that his mother isn't going to be able to finish his sweater after all. I don't want to buy him a sweater at Old Navy, so I read and reread the pattern trying to figure out if I've assembled the pieces in the wrong order. No, the ethereal flames didn't steer me wrong. The pieces are placed in the right order around the needle. I suspect that my impatience to finish the front piece Christmas afternoon may be what's causing the irregular neck. But I don't have the heart, or the skill, to unravel it and figure out what went wrong. I am stuck, utterly stuck.

It's time to go back to the Borealis Yarn store, back to Abby and her wooden table. I call over New Year's Eve weekend to see if they're open. No one answers, and the answering machine is full. I go online to see if they have a website. It's minimal, but at least the hours are posted. On Monday, I call to ask if this would be a good time to come in for a little help.

"Sure," says the young woman who answers the phone. "Come on over."

I hang up the phone, grab Evan's lumpy sweater, and head out into the balmy morning. The temperature has risen into the thirties. Instead of clean white snow and clear roads, we're stuck with slushy streets and gray soot coating the snowbanks that edge the city streets. When I reach the store, I spot the young woman I spoke to on the phone standing at the oval front table. She's marking down prices on a batch of knitting needles. Abby is over by the register. Today her short hair is dyed purple. She is wearing jeans and a Fair Isle pullover.

"I need help with my sweater," I say humbly as I set my knitted mess on the front wooden table. Abby makes a bee-line for the table and watches as I take out my work — the front and back threaded together on the circular needles.

"It just doesn't quite look right," I say, looking down, embarrassed. "I can't figure out what's wrong."

Then I address Abby: "I don't know if you remember this." I pull out the flame arms and the children's sweater pattern.

"Um-hmm," she says, acknowledging my project as she smoothes out the front and back pieces. "No, this isn't that bad. It's shaped right." She stretches it out to have a better look at how I've formed the neckline.

"Doesn't the neckline look weird? I just don't get how it all fits together."

"Let me see. Actually, it looks okay."

"Really? See, I've got the right number of stitches on the circular needle, but I think I kind of cheated."

"No, wait a minute," interrupts Abby. "What's going on here?"

The knitting shaman disappears again. Her tall frame, her

dazzling purple hair, her colorful sweater are standing eighteen inches in front of me. But she's gone completely silent, and her spirit has vanished. Abby has disappeared back down the rabbit hole and into the world of spirits and ancestral women of the cloth.

I stand beside her, awaiting her diagnosis. I'm uncomfortable with the silence. I want to interrupt her, but I don't. I turn around and look again at all the yarn in the store. This purview of paradise and promise has turned sour. I have forgotten all the joy of possibility and new beginnings that I once felt here.

"Okay, here's the deal," she says, returning to her body and the earth. Abby points to the pattern and shows me where I've gone wrong — at the point where I began shaping the neck in the front piece. Then she's cranky. She says, "How did you possibly get eleven stitches on each shoulder? You have to read the pattern. You can't cheat."

"I thought it was a matter of interpretation, kind of like rabbinical scholarship," I say.

Abby laughs. Good, the lecture is over. She pulls out the neckband and sets aside the back piece. Then she unravels the front piece until I'm back where I need to be, back at the beginning of shaping the neck. She shows me where I've gone wrong and tells me what I need to do. She rethreads the stitches onto my needle and hands it over. "Your turn."

"Okay, I think I've got it, but..." I pause, my face scrunched up almost ready to cry.

"Don't worry," she says. "You're not leaving here until you know how to finish this sweater."

She's right. Under her tutelage, with her assistant's help and my own work, I leave Borealis Yarns confident I can finish the sweater. But it takes a few hours.

I sit at the table in the front window where Abby first transformed the two sweater patterns into one that would fit Evan. Today, I reknit the front piece properly and bind it off again. No cheating. Then I start on the neck, placing the loose stitches from front and back pieces back onto the circular knitting needle. This time, the eleven stitches on either side of the front piece fall into place with ease.

While I mend the sweater, members of a knitting club come in together to pick up wool for their next project. Then a pair of opposites enters the shop — a thirty-something woman who wears the defiant, bald Sinead O'Connor look and an elderly woman who explains that she lives just a few blocks away. She's got a little too much makeup on her sagging face, and I can tell that her clothes have seen many Januaries before this one. Abby helps the younger woman, who, despite her fierce, intelligent look, seems to have a hard time keeping up with Abby's enthusiastic patter. Abby's assistant helps the elderly neighbor a few seats down from me at the wooden table.

"I know how to knit," announces the older woman, "as in knit one row and purl one row, but I've never started a pattern with a circle before, like this felt purse pattern my granddaughter gave me for Christmas."

A half-dozen other women — representing nearly all classes, shapes, and sizes — make their way in and out of the shop as I continue reknitting Evan's sweater. Whenever Abby and her assistant aren't helping these customers, they tidy up the shop. They rewind wool on pink-slippered Alex's yarn winder. They reorganize the front table. They mark down prices. They answer the phone. Then Abby admits that she hasn't had anything to eat yet today. So that's why she was a little edgy, I sigh. It wasn't that I broke the knitting rules. It turns out today is her day off, but one of her employees went home sick. The knitting shaman can't predict when she'll be needed.

After Abby returns from the coffee shop next door, presumably with a little food in her belly, she rejoins me at the table. I ask her how long she's been knitting. Since she was seventeen, she tells me. In her teens and twenties, she got retail experience working at a bookstore and at Sears. But this store is her first retail operation of her own. I think she's got a pretty good handle on running a successful business with heart. When I show her my finished, corrected front piece, she just smiles.

"And what about the arms?" I ask. "Do I sew them together before I sew them on?"

"No," she says again. She shows me how to fold the sleeves in half and line them up against the armhole before I start sewing. "Wow, this is really tight," she says as she tugs on the end of my emblazoned sleeves. "I just wonder if you oughtn't to unravel the sleeves and bind them off again more loosely. You know kids, if they try something on and it feels tight, they'll never wear it again."

She drops my sleeve to help another customer, and I watch the elderly lady pack up her felt-purse kit and leave the shop, ready to continue on her own. Abby asks her assistant to unpick the top of both of Evan's sleeves, pick up the stitches, and show me how to bind off with less tension. The assistant compliments me on the nice job I've done weaving in the loose ends of Evan's sleeves, because she can hardly find them. Then she teaches me two tricks. She shows me how to bind off loosely, forming the loops around two needles rather than just one. Second, she teaches me how to splice two pieces of wool together using spit and friction, by rubbing the two ends together in the palms of my hands until the two become one.

"Don't knit the neck too tight, either," says Abby as I open the door to leave. With new tricks, wider sleeves, and a neckband that I *can* knit, the rescue mission is complete.

Reluctance

"Want to go cross-country skiing, Andrew?" I ask my older son a few days later.

"No, Mom," he answers from his post, the couch where he's reading.

"How about you, Evan?" I persist, but he too declines.

"It'll be fun, guys. It's not too cold. Come on." Last winter I managed to get the boys cross-country skiing twice. This winter we're scoring zero, and it's already January.

"No, Mom," they say in unison.

Their reluctance isn't going to stop me. Promising the boys that we'll be back by noon, Diego and I load our cross-country skis into the back of the Honda. I set the poles in the rear and weave my skis over the back seat. The tips rest on top of the emergency brake. Guilt for not knitting follows me on this winter adventure — I swear the poles look like gigantic spindles for making yarn. The skis are really extra-long knitting needles. We head down the Montreal hill and land at our in-town ski destination, the city park that borders the river just below our house, just across from Pike Island.

After you learn how to balance and glide, cross-country skiing is blissful. As with knitting, once you get in a good groove, it feels like flying — not through the yarn, but on the surface of the snow. In no time you've unzipped your vest and stuffed your mittens into your pockets. You're sweating, but the cool breeze from cutting through the snow balances out the heat, like soaking in a hot tub outside in winter. Sometimes I want to ski all the way down the river to the Gulf of Mexico.

This is not one of those days.

Diego leans against the car in the parking lot to put on his gear. I carry mine to the nearby shelter. The temperature has been rising and falling this month, and there's a slick, crusty cover of ice on the ground. The groomed trail is going to feel like skiing on ice cubes. I click my boots into the bindings and bend my knees. Then, bam! I fall onto the hard-frozen ground. Unlike Evan, I do not think this is fun. I try hoisting myself back up, but each time I do, my skis inch farther away from my center of gravity — my bottom. It's almost comical, except that I'm mad.

"Are you all right?" asks Diego, skiing over to me. He hasn't seen the fall or my eventual recovery, but he can tell that I'm shaky.

"I don't know if I'm going to be able to do this."

"Do what?" he says, pulling off his Polarfleece cap, widening the opening at the top, and repositioning it on top of his sparse black and gray hair.

"Do what? Ski!" I huff and then push off in anger. I'm not angry at Diego. I'm angry at myself and my fear of the ice.

"Hey, wait a minute," calls Diego. "We don't have to ski. There aren't any rules about this, you know."

"Yeah, right," I mutter to myself as I go flying down a little hill that curves left, nearly falling again. My legs quiver harder. I hate this weakness in myself. So I keep going, my skis swishing in the trail grooves and weaving through the oak and pine forest until the river comes in sight. Today, the Mississippi is a sunny white ribbon. I stop and wait for Diego to catch up.

Diego believes goals are guides, not categorical rules. I disagree. Once you set a goal, you've got to reach the finish line. Right? Yet all kinds of hindrances have arrived this season. Grief from losing a good friend. Weakness when my period comes on strong. My domestic challenges at Christmas. My amateur standing as a knitter. Fear, like the dread of skiing on ice. I've completely forgotten that Evan's sweater is almost done.

Breathing the frosty air, I realize that sometimes I avoid pleasure just as easily as I avoid pain. I'll read four-fifths of a novel in a few days, but if I really like the book, it takes me another two weeks to finish. I'll design, plan, cultivate, and add compost in a garden in one weekend, but then wait a whole week before planting. I'll clean the bathroom meticulously, dreaming of soaking in a hot bubble bath, but then put off the bath.

I'm lingering at the end of Evan's sweater, too. It's not grief, or my period, or fear that's slowing me down. It's reluctance, pure and simple. I don't want to reach the end of doing something that, despite the hardships, has given me so much pleasure. It's because I'm so close to finishing it that I'm not knitting today. I'm skiing, or wobbling, on ice.

I'm not the only creator reluctant to see something end.

"Congratulations!" I told my friend Laura over the phone the other day. Laura and her husband relocated to Minnesota from Ireland two years ago. I had called to check in on their newborn. "A boy? Oh my gosh, you're going to have your hands full!"

When I ask her son's name, Laura says, "Funny you should ask that, Nora. Shall I tell you what I told my mum? I told her that we're going to follow the Chinese custom of waiting to name him until he turns one. That really wound her up. She practically hung up on me. My sister rang back to find out if we've gone off the deep end."

Laura is in no rush to name her new son. She has adapted to the northland. She knows how to hibernate in winter. She's already made one cocoon inside her body, and she knows that the baby's survival depends on staying cocooned inside her apartment this winter. But when you give a baby its name, the child gains a separate identity. The cocooning is over.

In knitting, the yarn is the umbilical cord — the lifeblood to creation. You've got to know when it's the right time to let go and snip the yarn, too. It's a balancing act between pleasure and pain.

I'm trying to balance pleasure and pain. In this season of a sweater, I've accepted many painful challenges, yet persevered. Sometimes it's better to take a break. But getting angry and pouting aren't graceful ways to pause.

"Hey, it's the marathon ski girl!" puffs Diego, reaching me here at the river. "Want to keep going?"

"No," I smile. "I can't stand all this ice. My legs won't stop shaking."

"Then let's turn around," he says sweetly.

We turn around and glide back over the icy tracks, away from the Mississippi. My legs stop wobbling on the return journey to the parking lot. I know why. My beloved partner is helping me learn how to balance. Not just on ice, but by balancing the goals we have set with honoring our heart. I don't have to be out here skiing today if it's too miserable. I can stay home and knit — or not knit.

This grace period, this gentle acceptance I find for myself seems to cure me and fills me with new energy. The next day, I drop off a baby name book with a thousand names for Laura and finish the neck of Evan's sweater.

Remembering Abby's advice, I add extra stitches around the neckline so that Evan won't be uncomfortable putting the sweater on and taking it off. The goldenrod circle opens wide like a wild lion's mane, reminiscent of Aslan from *Narnia*. The neckline is colorful, playful, and bold, perfect for the child of the lady who loved a multicolored mohair sweater. When I reach the last row of the neck, half of me wants to stop, but I don't. It's time to cut the umbilical cord. This baby is done.

Seams

It's 7:10 in the morning, dark, and cold. Andrew and I have both overslept, so I agree to give him a ride to school. While he readies his backpack, I wrap a winter jacket over my pink bathrobe. We head out the back door in silence across the crunchy, icy path to the garage. I back out into the slick alley. A blinding security light blinks on as we pass the garage two doors down. Andrew's face is illuminated briefly, and in that vanishing moment, I am not alone in the dark. I carry with me my family, my past, and my dreams for our future.

I make a U-turn in front of Andrew's school, hug him good-bye, and cut through the golf course for home. The sun is rising in the east over the river, over Pike Island. All that's visible is a soft pink glow hovering over the trees where Diego and I skied this weekend.

In the hour before I wake Evan up for school, I take out his sweater. It's time to sew in the sleeves. I thread a long piece of the charcoal gray yarn onto a thick sewing needle, turn the first sleeve inside out, and then stitch it up to form a tube.

By the time I'm done, it's almost 8:30. If I don't wake Evan up soon, he'll be late for school, too. But I'm driven to finish. I weave in the ends and thread a new piece of yarn to sew the second sleeve. Before I tackle it, I hear Evan in the bathroom upstairs. He pads downstairs and gives me a hug.

"I think I can finish your sweater tonight," I say. "You can wear it to school tomorrow."

"Really? Really, Mom?"

"You bet, kiddo," I say. "I think today's the day."

After walking Evan to school, I turn on the computer for a day of grant writing. There's good news from my colleague Shirlee about the art gallery. We were awarded two grants for City Indians, the art exhibit about the Dakota tribe's return to the Twin Cities in the 1950s.

"Score!" I say out loud to myself. Helping a nonprofit agency win a grant gives me a lift. It's kind of like finishing a knitting project. After all the effort, it's fantastic to cross the finish line. The rest of the day flies by.

Shirlee always says that things happen when they're meant to happen, even her grandson going off to Iraq. She'd probably say that I wasn't meant to finish Evan's sweater for Christmas. The universe has its own reasons to wait. It will be the right time to finish the sweater when all the necessary pieces show up — not a moment before that. I'm not sure if she's right, but by now I'm so excited about finishing that I've forgiven myself for missing my original deadline. As Diego would say, knitting a sweater shouldn't have to be accomplished by *any* damned deadline.

I sew up Evan's second sleeve after supper. Then I turn the whole sweater inside out and stitch up the side seams. I start at the bottom of the sweater on the right side and sew up to the armpit. The seam keeps going, curving around the armpit and back down the right sleeve. Second side. When I'm done, I call Evan over from the kitchen table.

"Are you ready?" I ask. Like a magician, I turn the whole sweater right side out.

Evan stares.

"Don't you want to try it on?"

"Okay, Mommy."

Evan threads his little arms through the ample sleeves. Then his head pops out of the king-sized golden neck. The sweater is on!

"Mom," he says, still staring at me. "Mom, I'm hot."

"Really?" I answer, worried that this is a bad thing — that he's already too hot and he'll never wear a wool sweater again.

"Yeah, I feel like I'm burning up like a supernova."

"Wow!" I say in relief, because for a seven-year-old boy, supernovas must be a good thing.

"Mom, do you know what a supernova is?"

"Sort of. A super-hot star, right?"

"Yeah, like the sun."

Close enough. Supernovas are exploding stars that are usually much larger and much hotter than our sun. I don't correct Evan. He's picked a good metaphor for the new sweater. He feels hot and powerful with it on. He's connected to the sun, carrying a bursting energy for the second half of winter.

The next morning goes smoothly. Andrew and I wake up in time for two rounds of Rummy 500 before he catches his bus. Ninety minutes later, Evan puts on his sweater and practically runs down the alley to school. When I pick Evan up that afternoon, I ask, "Did the kids like your new sweater?"

"Yeah, and Kenny, he asked if you would make him a sweater, too," he answers.

I laugh. Kenny is one of Evan's best pals at school. He is Hmong, and his grandfather is a shaman. Kenny's grandmother knows the power of the *paj ntaub* and the stories in each ancient flower cloth.

The story of Evan's sweater isn't part of the spirit world. It rests in the mundane world where I live with my children and with Diego in a skinny blue house by the river. Yet this sweater is sacred. I have had to dig deeply into the challenges of this season before I could complete it. It tells the story of all that has happened during one dark season in the northland. As it took shape, this sweater witnessed my sister's wedding on a sun-drenched early October day, two birthdays, one death, three holidays, and a birth. To make it, I called upon the wisdom of generations of women who've passed along the ancient traditions of making string, weaving, and knitting. To honor it, I lean in and listen.

Sledding

*L*istening doesn't come naturally to me. It requires resting and reflection. Our fast-paced American culture taught me to achieve goals by putting on blinders, blocking out distractions, and heading toward a finish line. I'm only beginning to understand that unexpected distractions provide texture and meaning to life's experiences. They steer us into whorls and eddies that force us to remember that the universe is much larger and stronger than any single goal. Listening reminds us that we walk on this precious earth together with all beings, not just as separate individuals.

Big things in nature remind me of this life lesson — a wild lightning storm in August, the river that wraps a moat around our hilly neighborhood in St. Paul. They force me to remember that my agenda isn't the only agenda to consider in a day. Knitting Evan's sweater has been full of unexpected distractions — my own limitations as a knitter, death and grief, celebrations and birth. As a result, bits of this winter's life experiences have been woven into the sweater. Its texture is richer, fuller, more human because of them. But to hear their lessons and to feel this texture, I've got to slow down and let go of my own agenda. I've got to be comfortable being still.

As January comes to a close, Evan and I invite my cousin Bridget and her first-grade daughter for dinner and sledding in our neighborhood at the Highland Park Golf Course. Bridget and I are only a month apart in age. We grew up more like sisters than cousins. Bridget is a knitter, too. She's always got a project or two going in the winter. When Andrew was little, she knit him a sweet toy clown with a slender, pointy cap. One of my fondest childhood memories is of playing outside with Bridget in the winter. Now it's our children's turn.

I mix up a batch of Swedish meatballs for later, then we all suit up. I put on a pair of thick snow pants and my winter jacket. Evan wears a pair of snow pants and his new sweater. "Not bad, eh?" I say pointing at the sweater and looking for feedback from my marvelous threesome. The sweater is warm, beautiful, functional, and a little funny looking with its extra-wide, lion's-mane neck. I love it.

"It's one of a kind," laughs Andrew, "like you, Mom."

"You know what," says Diego, "I am really proud of you. It's the most magnificent sweater I have ever seen."

I'm proud, too. I combined two patterns and then forged a few innovations of my own. That plus a lot of sweat, a rescue mission, and voilà — one sweater. Like life itself. We inherit patterns from our parents and then modify the patterns to suit new conditions and needs.

"Hey, when are you going to make me a sweater?" asks Andrew.

"You would never wear one — it's too scratchy."

"But you could make me something else," he smiles.

All four of us grab hats and step outside into the 10-degree afternoon. Diego and Andrew head off down the hill to a bookstore. Evan and I play outside. When our guests arrive, we've been moving around outside long enough that our warm layers are starting to feel like our own skin — comfortable and warm, impervious to the cold and wind. It's perfect for sledding. Bridget and I carry two yellow plastic sleds while the kids walk through the snowbanks. It's 5:30 by the time we reach our destination, and the sky is just turning a rosy pink. Evan's flames are doing their job. We will have light for another thirty minutes.

Evan and Eveline run up the hill and jump on their sleds. They shoot down the hill, leaving a trail of powder behind them. Evan shouts as he nears the end of his run. Eveline is quieter. Yet both of them hop out of their sleds at the end of the first run and march right back up the hill for more. Bridget and I perch on top of the highest hill, below one of the blue water towers. We cheer the kids on and talk about reading, writing, our children, and our relationships.

We have been chatting like this for decades. When we were in fourth grade, our Grandmother Murphy organized a book club for us. We'd meet at Great-Aunt Nora's apartment overlooking the Mississippi River, not far from this hill. We'd cozy into her couch and discuss great books like *Black Beauty* and *The Hobbit*. The greatest gift that their generation gave us was the sense that our ideas — and sharing those ideas — mattered. Bridget and I carry that gift with us wherever we go.

Today, where an outsider might see two women sitting on the crest of a sledding hill watching their children glide down the snowy slope on yellow plastic sleds, I see two mothers surrounded by the generation that gave us their love of language and the permission to gather together as women of consequence. I see two mothers who are trying to do the same for their children. However, we don't knit the exact same pattern that our mothers or grandmothers gave us.

We innovate. In some ways, Bridget and I are like the first mill workers in Lowell, experiencing a new kind of economic freedom. Yet we're also devoted mothers fiercely committed to creating a beautiful and safe world for our children. We're fashioning a new pattern. That doesn't mean we lose the responsibility for passing on the gifts we have been given.

The older generation hands off a needle lined with stitches. They pass along a pattern with directions. The new generation innovates, yet keeps the pattern going — like Betty, who learned to bead from an American Indian teacher at school, first by copying traditional patterns, then branching out to create her own designs. I was gifted metaphorical stitches and patterns from the women in my family. They modeled ways to knit, ways to celebrate Christmas, and ways to love the written word. Now, as a mother, it's my turn to pass on my stitches and pattern to Andrew and Evan. Dusk descends on this late January afternoon. Evan is wearing his new sweater. It's time to plan something to knit for Andrew, too.

As we head back home in the dusk, we're quiet. The sleds scratch against the thin layer of ice that forms at dusk when the top layer of snow, which has warmed in the afternoon sun, freezes again. We enjoy the warmth that spreads through our bodies, a warmth that comes from exerting ourselves in the cold. In this stillness, I realize something else. Yes, each item that we knit is textured with the life experiences that have surrounded us in the making. Yes, mothers like Bridget and I uphold the patterns we inherited and cast on new stitches for our children. But we are also the pattern itself.

Each one of us is a stitch in this bigger pattern of life's eddies. Each one of us is a stitch in the cosmic act of regeneration. Each stitch, each being, each act of existence is a part of this much bigger whole. The irony is that there's nothing special that we have to do to be a part of this pattern. We simply are. There are no goals to set, no deadlines to meet — or miss. Doubt, even stubborn self-doubt like mine, is irrelevant. Everything — every act we undertake, every misstep we make — is a perfect part of this universal weaving.

I have only a faint hold on this new realization. I sense it rather than understand it rationally. What I'm certain about is that the quiet of the dark season helped me begin to see the brilliance and power of this pattern. I am certain, too, that Evan's sweater is a part of it — not just the finished sweater, or any final product that a mother or aunt or friend knits for a child, but each stitch, each life experience, each inherited thread, each gift that gets passed on, are the infinite parts woven inside this larger pattern. I don't know who knits this gracious pattern; I only know that when I yield to its hold, a gentle beauty unfolds in my heart.

If I had finished Evan's sweater in time for Christmas, would I have grasped this design? Maybe I had to wait until the dark season began to lift to intuit the universal forces surrounding a simple sweater. The question is, can I keep my hold on this cosmic pattern and its gentle hum now that the light is growing and the days begin to stretch into spring?

Imbolc

"Mom, what are you doing with my sweater?" asks Evan.

I've pulled his sweater out of the basket in the back hall. I'm staring at it, fixated. In part because I'm amazed that I finished it; in part because I'm thinking about doing something else I've never done before.

It's the last day of January. Evan's sweater greeted us from the top of an unruly pile of winter gear when we walked in from school. Perched atop snow pants and hats, resting on Andrew's gray scarf and countless unmatched mittens, Evan's sweater is talking to me. I pick the sweater up and listen.

You're not done with me yet, it says.

Not done? What? I reply in silence.

I know exactly how to answer the sweater's invocation. To truly finish this sweater, I will call upon an ancient tradition. Not a tradition born out of the cradle of civilization birthed between the Tigris and Euphrates rivers where women first turned animal fibers into wool. Not a tradition born of the

Andean mountains or Mexican highlands where weaving and wool linked the community together. Not a tradition born in China, or Egypt, or the northeastern corner of South America, three places in the world where we know knitting began. Not even from my home on a hill above the confluence of the Mississippi and the Minnesota rivers where the Dakota were born.

To celebrate this evening, I call on Ireland, whose traditions my ancestors carried to this land. The Irish are famous for their cabled Aran sweaters, worn originally by fishermen on the western coast. But the links between Irish culture and textiles go much farther back in time.

Vestiges of goddess worship live on in Ireland. November 1 is All Soul's Day — a Catholic feast day honoring the dead. But All Soul's Day is really Samhain in disguise — the pagan festival that Andrew and I celebrated together at a bonfire many years ago in a St. Paul city park. Imbolc, the feast of Saint Brigid, arrives three months later.

On a visit to Ireland last year with the boys, Diego and I visited a sacred well devoted to Saint Brigid in County Clare. There, in a white humid grotto, thousands of women had come before us to say their prayers, seeking her healing, leaving behind photographs and medallions and ribbons and letters. In County Tipperary, we visited the cottage where my great-great-grandmother was born — the same great-great-grandmother who traveled up the Mississippi River in a steamboat to Minnesota. A Saint Brigid's cross, woven of straw, still hangs by my great-great-grandmother's cottage door.

Behind the Christian Saint Brigid stands a powerful Celtic goddess named Brigantia, whom the Christians adopted to help bring Christianity to Ireland. Brigantia represents an aspect of the mother goddess. Like Tlazolteotl from ancient Mexico, Brigantia represents the power of the mother goddess in midwinter or early spring, when the sun comes closer to the earth and the seeds in the ground are starting to stir.

Saint Brigid, like Brigantia before her, is the patroness of poetry, of fire, and of birth and healing. All four are connected with the changes in the land when February arrives. In Ireland, the ewes are starting to produce milk and are just about to give birth. Saint Brigid heals those in childbirth — the ewes and their lambs, cows and their calves, even humans and their babes. She does this by bringing them her fire energy.

Saint Brigid probably wouldn't recognize sheep farming and the wool industry today. Like American clothing, most of the yarn that American knitters buy today, even at independent shops like Borealis Yarns, comes from outside the country. Sometimes yarn travels across several borders before it reaches the United States. The wool from a herd of sheep living in Australia or New Zealand often moves across the ocean for processing in China. Distributors in Germany import the Chinese-spun yarn, then put their German labels on it for export to the United States.

Profit, as usual, is the motive for these journeys. It's not just about the price of labor or wool. Most American yarn-processing machines are outdated and slow, and more expensive to run than the newer machines in China and India. The Chinese are also innovative in their use of raw materials: they have figured out how to take the by-products of tofu and cornstarch production and turn them into yarns nearly as soft as silk. China also has the largest number of sheep in the world, though Australia, with the next-largest herd, produces more wool than any other country. U.S. textile production is dropping almost as fast as Chinese and Australian production is rising. In 1942, U.S. sheep producers cared for 56.2 million sheep. By 2001, the number had dropped to just 6.92 million. Even so, it's hard to imagine how Saint Brigid could watch over all these little lambs.

On one small sheep farm in southern Minnesota, the farmers shear their flock but discard the fleece because it would cost too much to process it into yarn. Their lambs become meat. But on small farms all around the country, some farmers are keeping alive Saint Brigid's art of caring for sheep and their wool. At Hollyhock Farm in central Minnesota, after the small flock of Icelandic sheep is sheared each spring, the shepherdess combines the top and bottom coats to make extra-durable wool. She then organizes the piles by fleece color: browns, grays, and creamy whites. Finally, she sends her annual clip to Michigan for processing into yarn. A simple skein of yarn from Hollyhock Farm retails for more than twenty dollars. That's still not enough for the shepherdess to make ends meet. She works a day job as a librarian in a nearby town.

In Ireland, women used to put a piece of cloth called the *brat bridh* outside on the night before Saint Brigid's Imbolc Feast. The next morning, they carried the cloth back inside, knowing that Saint Brigid had blessed it on her journey through the night. Like the ancient women of old Europe, the Irish women understood that this was no longer a scrap from an old dress or cloak: it was sacred and healing. In the year that followed, women would place the cloth on a mother — human or animal — in childbirth. The *brat bridh* carried Brigid's healing powers to ensure a safe birth. Life and cloth, the domestic and the sacred, are again entwined.

After the boys are in bed and Diego has turned off his

laptop and come upstairs, I tiptoe back down into the kitchen. I lift Evan's sweater from the heap of winter gear and hug it. I inhale the smell of the yarn, thick and alive with the residue of the sheep who once wore it. I put on my blue fuzzy birthday slippers and unlock the back door. It is so cold that my lungs hurt when I step outside.

"Good night," I say into the night air. With my eyes closed I linger outside for a moment, knowing in some strange way that my long-departed great-great grandmother, born in a cottage in Tipperary more than 150 years ago, is standing outside with me awaiting Saint Brigid's blessing tonight. I can't say how I know this, but for that frigid moment I am not alone — I am connected to the heart of a woman who, like me, hoped and knit and prayed for her children's safe passage. I set the sweater on the back railing, pat it for good luck, and step right back into the house.

The ancient Irish custom of linking sacred fabric with a safe birth for children and livestock isn't unique to Ireland. Rituals like the Irish *brat bridh* blessing probably first took place in Africa. Recall that the Yoruba women that traditionally sing to their mother goddess Iya Mapo for her blessing and protection when they dye their *adire* cloth indigo blue. The Kuba people of central Africa and the indigenous tribes in the Pacific Northwest all made special skirts and shawls to wear for ceremonial dances that marked powerful times of transition, including birth. Tunisian women clung to their ceremonial belts during childbirth, seeking Fatima's blessing.

This link between female divinity and powerful cloth appears in other parts of Europe, too. In Estonia, which sits across the Baltic Sea from the Scandinavian countries where the first sweaters were probably knitted, sacred birthing cloths were used for cattle. To heal livestock, Estonian families filled a left-hand knitted mitten with water and sprinkled the water over the sick cow in prayer, like a Catholic priest showering smoking incense over his congregation. When a young woman was married in Estonia, she wore a woven shawl to protect her groom's cattle from disease. As further protection, she wore a garter around her leg — a tradition carried on by many brides. As she neared her husband's home, the bride would drop the knitted garter onto the ground to protect her new family's cattle from getting sick. Just outside his house, she would sit down on a blanket and offer knitted mittens to her new family to increase their chances of fertility and good luck.

There's a big part of me that realizes that trying my hand at blessing Evan's sweater and making a modern-day *brat bridh* is a little silly. I'm not a pagan matriarch, I'm not 100 percent Irish, and I'm not a nineteenth-century Estonian bride or a Salish spinner. I'm a twenty-first-century white American mother who could have bought a sweater for Evan at Old Navy. Still, I am brushing off the dust that has accumulated over the centuries. I am sweeping out the debris that separates women today from the powerful connections that exist between cloth making and our regenerative powers — of healing, of fertility, of transformation.

The next morning, I get out of bed, put on my bathrobe, and head downstairs. I turn up the furnace and heat up a kettle of water for coffee. Then I open the back door.

It's colder this morning than last night. Much colder. My lungs ache even before the door is open all the way. Evan's sweater is still hanging on the back rail. The bright red and golden flames hint at warmth, but their fire isn't powerful enough to combat the bitter February morning air. I grab onto the door handle and reach as far as I can out to the back porch. Without taking a single step outside, I nab the sweater and slam the back door shut.

Back inside, I wonder if Saint Brigid has blessed our *brat bridh*. I hold the sweater up under the electric kitchen lights and investigate. It looks the same. It's colder, of course. Ah, but it smells different. There's a sweetness in the wool I didn't notice last night. The sweet smell reminds me of oatmeal cookies just out of the oven. I notice another difference, too. The sweater is quiet this morning. It has stopped talking, content to carry the silent strength of all the women — those here in St. Paul, those across time and place, and those in the spirit world like Saint Brigid — who helped bring it to life.

In this silence I realize that I've gone back to the very beginning of this winter story and back to the oldest known piece of cloth ever made by humans — a woman's skirt. By honoring the power of the cloth last night, I am calling back to the vestigial pagan goddesses across Europe who were worshipped with spinning whorls and miniature sculptures. I am calling back to the women in Mexico and in China, in the American Pacific Northwest, and in every corner of Africa. These women understood that making cloth, weaving, and knitting were physical manifestations of the greater pattern in life — a pattern that spins each simple stitch into a cosmic whole.

In these dark months of knitting Evan's sweater I've gotten a tiny glimpse into this bigger pattern. I've learned that each one of us who takes up knitting needles manifests life's pattern. We don't do this by force, or by rational decision. The stitches do the work for us. If we're quiet, we can hear the message of the stitches that have been handed to us. We can feel the stitches weave in life's joys and challenges. We can sense the patterns that our children will carry on. This is the cosmic pattern — this powerful act of regeneration.

If I could, I would walk across the street to an ancient weaving-goddess temple and sing a song of thanks, as did the ancient women of Europe. No such temple exists here, in our hilly river town. I'll have to improvise again. What I can do is give thanks for this newfound connection to the power of the cloth, right here at home. I give my *brat bridh* one last hug, thanking Saint Brigid, the goddess of fire and transformation, for her blessing. And I thank all the women around the world who've known that the power of turning string to cloth comes of its capacity to make visible the everlasting human desire to survive. Then I set the sweater back on the heap of winter gear to help guide my child's safe passage through the next year.

Epilogue

Threads of Time

When I began knitting Evan's sweater last October, I wasn't even sure I could finish it, let alone end up with so much more than a physical product. I discovered an ancient legacy from women who have clothed their families all over the globe.

They are the ordinary women who first turned flax and wool into yarn, and yarn into knitted socks. They are Saint Brigid and the goddesses Ishtar, Tlazolteotl, and Iya Mapo. They are the ancient Salish spinners and the knitting Madonnas who showed us that making clothing is divine.

They are artists who keep vestiges of the goddess alive, like the Hmong women who carried the brightly colored *paj ntaub sev* through China and to America. They are the artists who keep cultures alive, like Betty and Janet, whose floral beadwork and medicine wheels keep Ojibwe patterns whirling, yet centered.

They are the named and unnamed women who sweated and still sweat to make our clothes — the Greek slaves, the daughters of Mexico, the English peasants, the immigrants from Italy, the Estonian brides, the Hmong ball tossers, and the Honduran maquiladoras. They are the knitting shamans, like Abby, who travel to the spirit world to bring order back into the mundane world.

Each one of these women has left a stitch, a pattern, a thread, a story that belongs to those of us who knit today. They give us experience, wisdom, and the beauty of their craft. We are the ordinary, yet extraordinary, heroes who are keeping the heritage alive.

Last October I started a difficult project. I needed help from all these women to knit Evan's sweater. In the process, I learned how important textiles are for human survival. By clasping my knitting needles and persevering along the bumpy road to the finished sweater, I learned that I, and all of us who knit today, belong in this global pantheon of women crafters.

By telling this story of Evan's sweater, and of the women across time and all over the globe who helped me finish it, I also learned that it's our turn to take up the needles and keep the patterns going. The Inca *quipu* knotters, the African appliqué artists, the Hmong *paj ntaub* stitchers, the Meso-potamian tablet writers, and Saint Brigid's bards understood this. Now we're the ones with the knowledge to share and pass on to the next generation.

Our stories and our craft tell us who we are and where we've been. Without the story or the craft, we lose the legacy. Even Alice in Wonderland understood that once she came back up the rabbit hole it was her turn to tell the story. If we don't tell these stories, if we don't join this circle, our precious fiber heritage and the rich connections between women and the cloth might disappear like lost threads.

Each stitch matters.

Our stitches matter especially during the times of transition when economic changes challenge our divine work. Centuries ago, the Greek and English factories took away women's power to create their own cloth. Today, the global sweat-ers are the young women like Yesenia and Camella, who toil away in garment factories where they are underpaid and overworked. We can honor these women of the past and of today by acknowledging their pain. At the same time, we can help shift the balance in the global economy by creating our own clothing made from local goods. Knitting a single sweater won't shift the balance toward justice, but thousands of sweaters just might. Gandhi changed a nation with the call to spin cotton. These days, Evo Morales is working to change another wearing his alpaca sweater. We don't have to be national heroes to make change, either. By acknowledging the challenges that surround us, by listening and honoring the earth's cycles, we can find new wisdom to share in our ordinary lives.

Economic injustices aren't the only challenge to my own knitting, especially this time of year. As Saint Brigid's fiery energy increases through the springtime, I won't want to sit by my chair at the fire after dinner. I'll be itching to get outside and feel the sun on my body. Evan's sweater will sit for months at the back of his closet. It won't be long before we bike around the block in short sleeves and check out the lilacs, not quite believing that they will bud and blossom. They will, and before long it will be time to plant and tend Evan's pumpkin seeds. At the summer solstice, Diego and I will take Evan back down the hill and over the river to Lake Nokomis, Grandmother Lake.

But I haven't hung up my needles yet. Now I vow to knit

Andrew something that won't aggravate his allergies, something not too scratchy. Mittens. I email my friend Elizabeth and ask her to suggest a pattern. Then, on a drive to Moose Lake, two hours north of St. Paul, I discover a new yarn store that specializes in American-made wool. I splurge on two skeins from the producer, Hollyhock Farm — a soft poplar gray and a flecked, creamy white. On a whim, I drive east out of town to visit the farm. Jeanne, the shepherdess, is at work today, but her husband agrees to show me her flock of fourteen Icelandic sheep — one of the world's oldest breeds of sheep, only recently introduced to the United States.

He takes me into the barn where the sheep are having an early-afternoon nap. "This is LuLu," he says, petting a mocha brown sheep who walks over to nuzzle him. "And that's Ruthie, with the lighter brown coat. She's the mother of most of them." Ruthie is lying down. She twists her head while chewing hay. Her top and bottom jaws don't meet, so she looks like the talking Ma in the movie *Babe*.

"Who's that one over there, standing away from the group?" I ask, as we walk deeper into the barn, over the hay-strewn floor.

"The one that looks like a sweater?" he squints and tilts his head. We both stare at this solitary sheep with the mottled brown and white face and tan checkered coat. "That's Molly. She thinks she's smarter than the rest of them. When the vet comes, she thinks she doesn't need any shots."

Jeanne has raised this small flock for about seven years. Every skein of yarn costs her money. It's a labor of love. In the winter months, her husband confesses, "Sometimes I find Jeanne fast asleep in the barn, nestled in with the sheep as blankets." In the summer, she turns their fleece into sturdy, beautiful yarn that combines the sheep's thick undercoat with the more durable outer coat, or guard hair. The sheep whose fleece Jeanne prefers for her own knitting is Nickie. I pet Nickie and find her coat is full, soft, and airy, reminding me of the thick fuzzy slippers Evan gave me in November.

"He's dark brown on the top, but a really creamy tan underneath," I notice.

"That's right. You can't tell their color just by the top coat. What color did you say you bought at the shop in town?" asks Jeanne's husband, offering Nickie a handful of grain.

"I bought two — a light creamy color and a soft gray."

"Well, it's hard to say which sheep made the creamy white, but gray?" he bends down on one knee to feed the others, who've nuzzled Nickie out of the way. "That's got to be Molly. She's a tan patchwork quilt on the top, but she's got a beautiful gray undercoat."

When I get home, I pull off the hand-decorated label and unwrap Molly's wool. The twisted skein opens into a circle, into *the* circle that connects us in this ancient art. I loosen the ends and discover that this yarn is made of two plies. They are twined like the two rivers and the two waters that birthed the Dakota right below our house and the cradle of civilization halfway around the world in Iraq. Like the yarn that the world's first knitters in Egypt formed into sacred socks and the first knitters in South America used to make belts to protect the wearer's inner organs. Like the mixture of mud and vegetables women still use to dye *bogalanfani* in West Africa, and like the cedar and animal fur the Salish Indians use to weave magical blankets.

If beginnings are bliss, reaching the end is hard work. I've dropped more stitches than I care to admit, but I've gained faith in myself this season. If I don't finish Andrew's new mittens before the snow melts in March, I know I'll have a great present for my wiseacre son next Christmas — mittens from Molly, the sheep who thinks she's too smart to join the crowd.

I unravel the primordial circle slowly, enjoying the smell and vibrant texture of this two-ply yarn. I press yarn into a thick ball like a snowball. It responds, bouncing back — alive with pure energy, born of the hay and love and long dark winter months that nursed the sheep and its wool on a nearby farm.

Gone is the self-doubt that's plagued me all through Evan's sweater this winter. I've learned that self-doubt lingers when we keep ourselves isolated. I'm no longer alone; I'm in the company of many good women. I'm part of a pattern that will keep weaving a larger whole whether I want to participate or not. I am surrounded by the protective energies of the earth, where we can burrow to find nutrients in the soil and wisdom for the heart. This protective energy begins right here at home in the dark season — here in a skinny blue house overlooking the sacred birthplace of the Dakota.

I believe it's no accident that the Dakota tell the story of an old woman who sits in a cave warmed by a fire. Her companions are a dog and a blanket she is quilling. The three of them have sat by this fire in this cave for at least a thousand years. Each time the old woman rises to put wood on the fire and stir her red berry soup, the dog undoes her quillwork. Like Penelope in Greece, the Dakota woman must begin again, reworking the quill design into the blanket when she returns to her seat by the fire. The Dakota say that if this ancient woman should ever stop her quillwork, the world would come to an end. We are indebted to her for our very lives.

If the lessons I've learned during this dark season in the northland are true, I don't think the woman quills, or knits, only out of duty. She works her needles with the deep love that a mother has for a child. As the blanket, or the sweater, emerges, she gives birth to the abiding love that protects us all.

When I cast on this time, I call in the sacred string that connects the past and the future — right here, right now. I use a magic trick I learned at Borealis Yarns during this dark winter. Instead of starting over again from scratch, I'm going to splice together two threads of time. In one hand, I put the magnificent legacy of women and textiles — from down the hill at the confluence of the Mississippi and Minnesota rivers, and from all around the world. In my other hand, I put the exuberant energy of beginning a new project. I overlay the two pieces — the past and the future — spit into them like a llama, and start rubbing them together in the palm of my hands. The single string that emerges is the love that knits the universe into being. With it, I sit back in my comfy chair by the fire, ready to keep knitting.

Acknowledgments

$\mathcal{K}$ nitting *the Threads of Time* weaves together my best attempt to share the joy of knitting for my children with the gifts so many people have given me through their stories, life experiences, and hard-earned wisdom. Any mistakes in the translation, of course, are mine. I would like to express my gratitude —

To those who taught me how to knit: my mother, Sandra Murphy, and Abby Lamberton at Borealis Yarns.

To the knitting designers April Fischer and Melissa Leapman, whose patterns I modified to knit Evan's sweater ("Jesse's Flames," created by April Fischer, in *Stitch 'n' Bitch Nation*, by Debbie Stoller [New York: Workman Publishing, 2004], and "Rugby Stripe," designed by Melissa Leapman [Mitchell, NE: Brown Sheep Company, Inc., 1997]).

To those who shared their stories with me: Tania Forte, Tyrone Guzmán, Chris Leith, Betty Moore, Elizabeth Morrison, Bee Moua, Bridget Murphy, Janet Boswell, Shirlee Stone, Laura Whitley-Mott, and Pa Dee Yang.

To those who provided excellent historical guides: Juanita Espinosa, Native Arts Circle; Dr. Gary Yia Lee, Center for Hmong Studies, Concordia College; Patty Martinson, Minneapolis Institute of Arts; Linda Knudsen McAusland; Deborah Ramos; and my father, John Murphy.

To the local farmers who showed me how North Americans are reviving small-scale fiber farms: Jeanne and Dick Coffey of Hollyhock Farm, Wendy Guck, and Judy Nielson of StoneCroft Alpacas.

To those who read the manuscript with care and compassion: Kate Bjork, Roxana Linares, Lisa Van de Steur, Chan Vang, and my sister, Cate Murphy.

To the people who wrote early endorsements for the book: Heid Erdrich, Lawrence Sutin, Diane Wilson, and Lee Pao Xiong.

To those who gave me a wonderful space to write: the Jerome Foundation and the Blacklock Nature Sanctuary.

Special thanks to my energetic agent, Kate Epstein; kindhearted editor Georgia Hughes; and all the staff behind the scenes at New World Library.

Finally, my thanks to those who are my daily inspiration — my beloved Diego Vázquez and my magnificent boys, Andrew and Evan.

Bibliography

African Textiles

Brooks, Conan. "Introduction to Kuba Weavings." Antiquarius Imports Lecture Series. www.antiquariusimports.com/lectures-kuba-weavings.php (accessed September 9, 2008).

Gillow, John. *African Textiles*. San Francisco: Chronicle Books, 2003.

Jones, Kimberly Michelle. "History, Origin and Significance of Mud Cloth." John Henrik Clarke Africana Library. www.library.cornell.edu/africana/about/mudcloth.html (accessed September 9, 2008).

Renne, Elisha. "'Our Great Mother...Tied This Cloth': Pelete Bite Cloth, Women and Kalabari Identity." In *Cloth is the Center of the World: Nigerian Textiles, Global Perspectives*, ed. Susan J. Torntore. St. Paul, MN: Goldstein Museum of Design, 2001.

Runge, Emily. "African Adire Cloth." Charlotte Country Day School's World Cultures Resources website, www.ccds

.charlotte.nc.us/History/Africa/save/runge/runge.htm (accessed May 15, 2008).

Stone, Caroline. *Embroideries of North Africa*. New York: Longman, 1985.

Wolff, Norma. "'Leave Velvet Alone': The Adire Tradition of the Yoruba." In Torntore, ed., *Cloth is the Center of the World*.

Asian Textiles

Murphy, Nora. *A Hmong Family*. Minneapolis, MN: Lerner Publications, 1997.

"Prehistoric Chinese City Brought to Light." China.Org.Cn, July 29, 2002. www.china.org.cn/english/culture/38057.htm (accessed September 9, 2008).

North American Textiles

Erdoes, Richard, and Alfonso Ortiz, eds. *American Indian Myths and Legends*. New York: Pantheon Books, 1984.

Farley, Harriet. "Letters from Susan: Fourth Letter," *Lowell Offering* 4 (September 1844): 257–59.

Gibson-Roberts, Priscilla. *Salish Indian Sweaters: A Pacific Northwestern Tradition*. Saint Paul, MN: Dos Tejedoras Fiber Arts Publications, 1989.

Halliday, Jan. "The Case of the Exploding Knitting Needle," *Port Townsend and Jefferson County Leader*, August 11, 2004, www.ptleader.com/print.asp?ArticleID=10138&SectionID=36&SubSectionID=55.

History Matters: The U.S. Survey Course on the Web, American Social History Project/Center for Media and Learning, City University of New York and Center for History and New Media at George Mason University, http://historymatters.gmu.edu/d/61 (accessed August 15, 2008).

Jack, Joe. "Coast Salish Spindle Whorl." www.joejack.com/salishspindlewhorl.html (accessed August 19, 2008).

Lalish, Paula. "The Case of the Exploding Knitting Needle," www.paulalalish.com/needle.htm (accessed 10/29/08).

"Lowell National Historical Park: Decline and Recovery," Lowell National Historical Park, www.nps.gov/archive/lowe/loweweb/Lowell_History/decline.htm (accessed August 15, 2008).

Lyford, Carrie A. *Ojibwa Crafts*. Stevens Point, WI: R. Schneider Publishers, 1982.

————. *Quill and Beadwork of the Western Sioux*. Boulder, CO: Johnson Books, 1979.

Old Sturbridge Village, Inc., website. www.osv.org.

Parsell, Diana. "Remnants of the Past: High-Tech Analyses of Ancient Textiles Yield Clues to Cultures." *Science News Online*, December 11, 2004. http://findarticles.com/p/articles/mi_m1200/is_24_166/ai_n12417198 (accessed August 19, 2008).

"Scraps of Prehistoric Fabric Provide a View of Ancient Life," Ohio State University Research News, August 22, 2004, http://researchnews.osu.edu/archive/prefab.htm (accessed September 3, 2008).

Tedlock, Barbara. *The Woman in the Shaman's Body*. New York: Bantam Books, 2005.

Teller, Adam, and Grandma Thompson. "Spider Woman and the Holy Ones." www.canyondechelly.net/story_teller (accessed August 19, 2008).

Williams, Suzi Vaara. "A Chilkat Weaving Adventure: A Month of Summers." http://alaskanativearts.net/suzi/chilkat.htm (accessed August 19, 2008).

————. "The Essence of Chilkat Weaving." http://alaska nativearts.net/suzi/essence.htm (accessed August 19, 2008).

———. "Tlingit Textiles." http://alaskanativearts.net/suzi /tlingit.htm (accessed August 19, 2008).

Yafa, Stephen. *Big Cotton: How a Humble Fiber Created Fortunes, Wrecked Civilizations, and Put America on the Map*. New York: Viking, 2005.

European Textiles

Adovasio, J. M., Olga Soffer, and Jake Page. *The Invisible Sex: Uncovering the True Roles of Women in Prehistory*. New York: Smithsonian Books, 2007.

Angier, Natalie. "Furs for Evening, but Cloth Was the Stone Age Standby." *New York Times*, December 14, 1999.

Barber, Elizabeth Wayland. *Women's Work: The First 20,000 Years*. New York: W. W. Norton, 1994.

Bower, Bruce. "Stone Age Fabric Leaves Swatch Marks: Imprints of Oldest Known Woven Material Found at Pavlov I site in Czech Republic." *Science News*, May 6, 1995. http://findarticles.com/p/articles/mi_m1200/is_n18 _v147/ai_16858571 (accessed August 19, 2008).

Bush, Nancy. *Folk Knitting in Estonia*. Loveland, CO: Interweave Press, 1999.

Forero, Juan. "The Fashion of the Populist." *New York Times*, February 2, 2006.

Fowler, Brenda. "Find Suggests Weaving Preceded Settled Life." *New York Times*, May 9, 1995.

Gimbutas, Marija, and Miriam Robbins Dexter. *The Living Goddesses*. Berkeley: University of California Press, 1999.

Montgomery, D. H. "The Leading Facts of English History." http://hcoop.net/~ntk/englishhistory.txt (accessed August 19, 2008).

Rutt, Richard. *A History of Hand Knitting*. Loveland, CO: Interweave Press, 1989.

Soffer, O., J. M. Adovasio, and D. C. Hyland. "The 'Venus' Figurines: Textiles, Basketry, Gender and Status in the Upper Paleolithic." *Current Anthropology* 41, no. 4 (August–October 2000).

Sundbø, Annemore. *The History of Norwegian Lace Patterns.* Norway: Torndal Twel, 2001.

Wright, Mary. *Cornish Guernseys and Knit-Frocks.* London: Ethnographica, 1979.

Latin American Textiles

Anwalt, Patricia Rieff. *Indian Clothing before Cortés: Meso-american Costumes from the Codices.* Norman: University of Oklahoma Press, 1981.

"Caral: Ancient Peru City Reveals 5,000-year-old 'Writing.'" *South African Broadcasting News,* July 19, 2005.

Seiler-Baldinger, Annemarie. *Maschenstoffe in Sud und Mittel-amerika.* Basel, Switzerland: Pharos Verlag H. Schwabe AG, 1971.

Solid, Shady Ruth, Jonathan Haas, and Winifred Creamer. "Dating Caral, a Preceramic Site in the Supe Valley on the Central Coast of Peru." *Science* 292, no. 5517 (April 17, 2001).

Tedlock, Barbara. *The Woman in the Shaman's Body.* New York: Bantam Books, 2005.

Yafa, Stephen. *Big Cotton: How a Humble Fiber Created Fortunes, Wrecked Civilizations, and Put America on the Map.* New York: Viking, 2005.

Middle Eastern Textiles

Barber, Elizabeth Wayland. *Women's Work: The First 20,000 Years.* New York: W. W. Norton, 1994.

Burnham, Dorothy K. "Coptic Knitting, an Ancient Technique." *Textile History* 3 (1972).

Levey, S. M. "Illustrations of the History of Knitting Selected from the Collection of the Victoria and Albert Museum." *Textile History* 1, part 2 (1969).

Lilinah biti-Anat. "Dar Anahita: Medieval Egyptian Knitting 1." http://home.earthlink.net/~lilinah/Knitting/Egypt Knit1.html (accessed August 19, 2008).

Scarce, Jennifer. "Summary of Paper on Medieval Middle Eastern Knitting," Early Textile Study Group, Manchester 2004. www.knittinghistory.co.uk/archive/summaryscarcej 2004.html (accessed August 19, 2008).

Speiser, A., and George A. Barton. *Archeology and the Bible.* 7th ed. Philadelphia: American Sunday School Union, 1937.

"Tricots." In *Tissus d'Égypte, témoins du monde arabe VIIIe–XVe siècles.* Collection Bouvier. Geneva: Musées d'Art et d'Histoire; Paris: Institut du Monde Arabe, 1993.

Woolley, Linda. "The Bouvier Collection: Medieval Arab-Islamic Textiles." *Hali, The International Magazine of Antique Carpet and Textile Art* 76 (August–September 1994).

The Contemporary Textile Industry

"Australia's Wool Industry." *WoolFacts.* September 2005. www.wool.com.au

Dodd, Erin, and William Oxenham. "Outlook for the U.S. Short-Staple Yarn Industry." *Journal of Textile and Apparel, Technology and Management* 2, no. 3 (Summer 2002).

Featherstone, Liza, and United Students against Sweatshops. *Students against Sweatshops.* London: Verso, 2002.

SID: Sheep Production Handbook, vol. 7. Centennial, CO: American Sheep Industry Association, Inc., 2002.

Other

Sarton, May. *Journal of a Solitude.* New York: W. W. Norton, 1973; reprint, 1992.

Index

About the Author

Nora Murphy is a freelance writer who specializes in writing for community-based nonprofit organizations in Minneapolis and St. Paul. She is the author of several children's history books and a coauthor of *Twelve Branches* (Coffee House Press, 2003), a collection of short stories that was a finalist for the Minnesota Book Award. Her essays have appeared in numerous journals, including *A View from The Loft* and *Minnesota History*. She is a graduate of the University of Chicago and holds an MFA in writing from Hamline University. She received a Blacklock Nature Sanctuary Writing Fellowship in 2006 from the Jerome Foundation to write *Knitting the Threads of Time*. Murphy is also a writer-in-residence with COMPAS Writers and Artists in the Schools. She is currently working on a book about the impact of the European conquest of Native lands, with a focus on her Irish Potato Famine ancestors' homestead in central Minnesota. A novice knitter, she lives in St. Paul with her family. For more information, please visit www.nora-murphy.com.